What you eat directly affects your health. Food Power explains simply and clearly why we should eat more of some foods and less of others.

food power

Food Power has been specially created for Tesco.

Consultant editors: Ann F. Walker (Nutritionist and Medical Herbalist) BSc MSc PhD MNIMH MCPP FRSH MIBiol MIFST and Alan L. Lakin BSc MSc PhD CChem FRSC FRSH MIFST

First published in 2000 by
Tesco Stores Limited
Created by Brilliant Books Ltd
84-86 Regent Street
London W1R 5PA

Origination by Colourpath Ltd, London
Printed and bound by Butler and Tanner, England

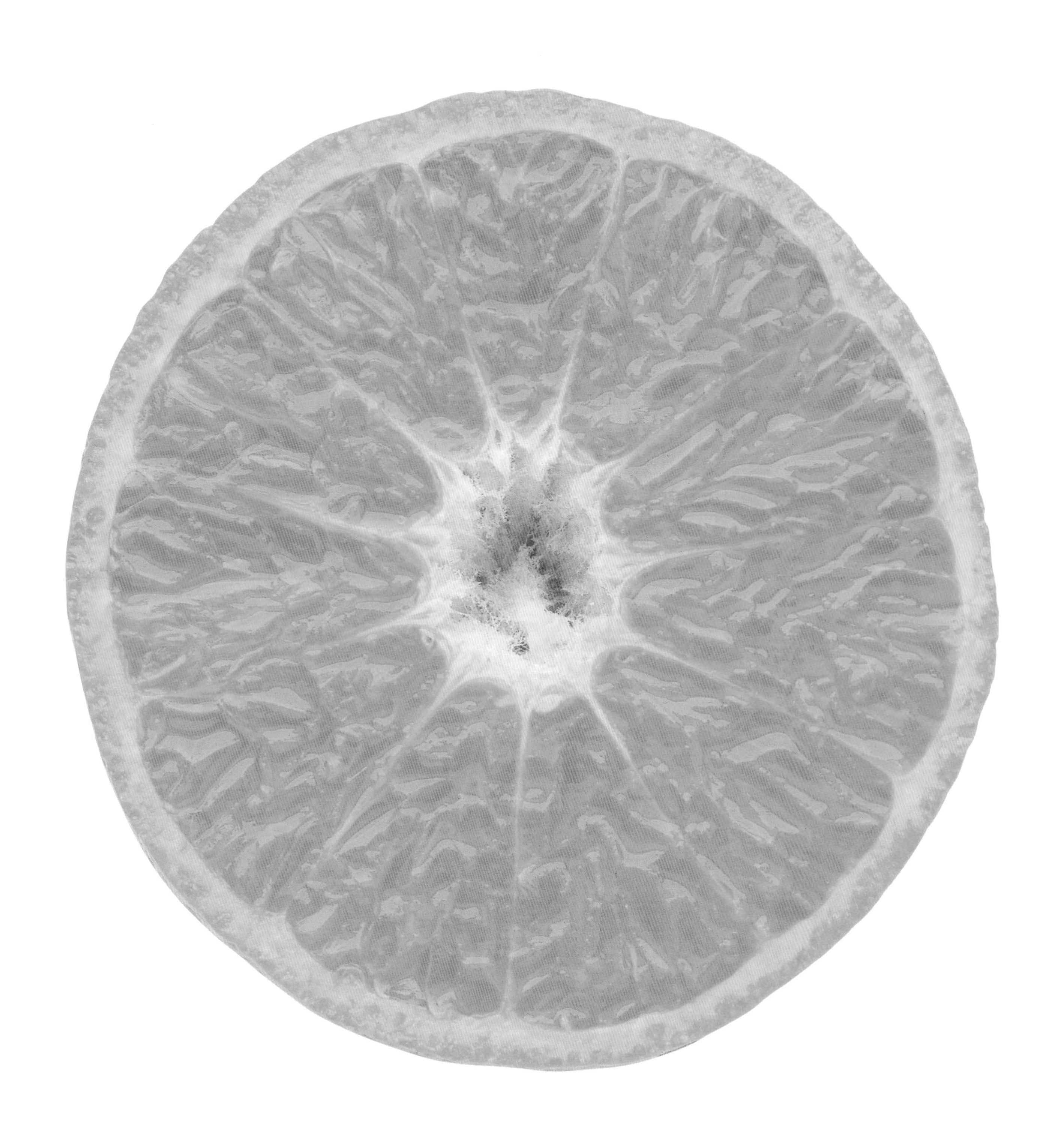

where to start

Every day we make choices about what to eat and drink, which directly affect our health. The aim of this book is to help you choose a well-balanced and varied diet and so enjoy a healthier life.

Food Power is an A-Z guide to foods and ailments. You can look up an entry on an individual food and see what vitamins, minerals and other nutrients it contains. You can also look up an ailment, and find out which foods may help to cure, or at least alleviate, the condition. *Food Power's* practical advice is supported by evidence from orthodox and traditional medicine.

A balanced diet doesn't just boost your body's ability to fight off colds and other infections, it can also help to combat stress, insomnia and low energy levels. And in the long term, eating sensibly can help reduce the risk of serious illnesses such as cancer and heart disease.

Nutrition is still a young science: barely a month goes by without new discoveries hitting the headlines, and many of us feel overwhelmed with seemingly conflicting information. This book will help you to cut through the confusion. It tells you what you need to know about subjects such as fats, cholesterol and antioxidants, and it examines controversial issues such as the safety of genetically modified foods.

Food Power will enable you to make informed choices about healthy eating for you and your family. It will help to ensure that your diet provides everything you need to live life to the full.

Using this book

Many foods are described as 'excellent', 'rich', 'good' or 'useful' sources of certain nutrients. These descriptions relate to the Department of Health's recommended daily requirements: 'excellent' means a serving provides the full adult requirement, 'rich' three-quarters, 'good' a half, and 'useful' a quarter. A food said to 'contain' a nutrient supplies one-eighth or more of the adult daily need. One Calorie (with a capital 'C') is equivalent to 1kcal or 1,000 calories (with a small 'c'). Most food labels use kcals – not Calories. Cross references, shown in SMALL CAPITALS, refer you to related entries, while at the back of the book you will find an index as well as a list of helpful organisations.

They keep food safe for longer, improve its quality and increase its appeal. But do additives pose a health threat?

additives

benefits

1 Help prevent food from spoiling.

2 Improve the appearance and the taste of food.

3 Help to ensure we derive the maximum nutritional benefit from our food.

drawbacks

1 Colourings and flavourings can increase the appeal of foods with little nutritional value.

2 A few people react adversely to additives such as benzoic acid, sulphites and tartrazine.

safety first

No additive is harmful in itself. But for a small minority of people certain additives may be hazardous to health. If you think you may be sensitive to one, check with your doctor.

Despite what many people think, the health advantages of additives in our food far outweigh the hazards. Natural and synthetic additives account for less than 0.5 per cent of all the food we eat, and only one person in 1,800 has definitely been shown to have an adverse reaction to synthetic additives. But many people are still worried about a possible link between additives and ALLERGIES.

The use of all additives except artificial flavourings (of which there are more than 3,000) is controlled by law. To be approved, they must be shown to be safe, effective and necessary, and be listed on packaging.

Additives have many different functions. Preservatives protect food from bacterial contamination and prolong shelf life. Occasionally, they can have adverse effects on our health: benzoates (used to slow deterioration) and sulphites (used to kill yeasts that spark sugar fermentation in food and alcohol) can – in rare instances – trigger allergic reactions.

Exposure to oxygen in the air makes fruit and fruit juices turn brown, and fats and oils go rancid – unless ANTIOXIDANTS are

Colouring is added to squash to make it look bright orange – the colour consumers think it ought to be.

introduced to slow down the process. Vitamin C (ascorbic acid or E300) is often added to fruit, while gallates are added to prevent fats turning rancid.

Colourings are often used to make food look more appetising to consumers – we expect orange squash to look orange and margarine to look yellow. The yellow colouring tartrazine (E102) has been linked with asthma attacks and hyperactivity in a few susceptible children.

Flavour enhancers are found in savoury foods. Monosodium glutamate (MSG) is still often blamed for allergic reactions such as swelling of the lips and vomiting, but the real culprits are now thought to be fermented soya and shellfish sauces, which are also often used in Chinese cooking.

Emulsifiers and stabilisers prevent oils and water separating out. Thickeners and gelling agents improve texture and consistency in foods like yogurts and ice cream.

Non-sugar sweeteners, such as sorbitol and xylitol, are used in sugar-free sweets and diabetic jams, and have roughly the same number of calories as sugar. There have been claims of adverse effects from the artificial sweeteners saccharin, aspartame and acesulfame-K, in low-calorie products, but so far none has been proven.

all about additives

additives	used in	why they're used
PRESERVATIVES Nitrites and nitrates (E249-52)	Sausages, bacon, other processed meats.	To prolong shelf life and protect food from fungi and bacteria. Nitrites and sulphur dioxide also function as colour preservatives. Ascorbic acid stops fruit juices turning brown, and fatty foods from going rancid. It also boosts the baking quality of wheat. In rare instances, sulphur compounds may cause allergic reactions, such as asthma.
Benzoic acid and benzoates (E210-19)	Soft drinks, beer, salad cream.	
Sulphur dioxide and sulphites (E220-28)	Dried fruit, desiccated coconut, fruit-based pie fillings, relishes.	
ANTIOXIDANTS Ascorbic acid/ascorbates (E300-4)	Fruit juices, fruit jams, tinned fruit.	
BHA/BHT (E320-21)	Fruit pies, crisps, biscuits.	
COLOURINGS Tartrazine (E102) Quinoline (E104) Sunset yellow (E110) Beetroot (E162) Caramel (E150)	Processed foods, including confectionery, soft drinks, jams, margarine.	To make food more visually appealing. Some may trigger allergic reactions such as wheeziness in asthmatics or hyperactivity in children.
FLAVOUR ENHANCERS Monosodium glutamate or MSG (E621) Monopotassium glutamate (E622) Disodium inosinate (E631)	Chinese food, stock cubes, gravy powders, packet soups, tinned and processed meats.	To make many tinned and processed foods taste better. Claims that MSG triggers allergic reactions have not been scientifically proven.
EMULSIFIERS, STABILISERS, THICKENERS Guar gum (E412) Gum arabic (E414) Pectins (E440) Cellulose (E460) Lecithin (E322) Glycerol (E422)	Breads, biscuits and cakes, sauces and soups, frozen desserts, ice cream, margarine and other spreads, jams, chocolate, quick-setting desserts, milk shakes.	To improve texture of food, making it appear more substantial, smoother and creamier. They also stop oil and water from separating out into layers.

A little alcohol really can be good for you – health risks only begin to stack up if you drink too much

alcohol

benefits

1 For older men and women, moderate levels of drinking can reduce the risk of coronary heart disease.

2 Drinking in moderation can be enjoyable and help people relax.

drawbacks

1 Too much alcohol raises blood pressure; this can increase the risk of coronary heart disease and strokes.

2 Regular high intakes may cause liver damage and cirrhosis of the liver.

3 High intakes are linked with increased risk of certain cancers.

4 It is hazardous during pregnancy.

5 It is harmful if mixed with certain drugs.

Most people enjoy drinking alcohol, and find it relaxing and sociable. But heavy drinking and alcoholism are quite common causes of illness and death. So where do the benefits end and the risks begin?

The main active ingredient (and health hazard) in all alcoholic drinks is ethanol. This is made by yeast fermentation of sugar or starch – a process that also forms substances called congeners, which give drinks their specific taste and aroma. Unfortunately, they can also be responsible for hangovers, and aggravate the dehydration effects caused by the alcohol itself.

Alcohol is normally absorbed into your bloodstream between 15 and 90 minutes after drinking, depending on your size, weight and how much you have drunk. Drinking on a full stomach can delay the absorption time. Spirits and fizzy drinks – such as champagne or sparkling cider – are absorbed more quickly.

Once in the bloodstream, some alcohol is released into the air through the lungs, but most of it goes to the liver, which takes about an hour to break down and remove just one unit of alcohol (see the chart on page 10). So if you are drinking alcohol late into the evening, you could still be over the legal limit for driving the following day, even after several hours of sleep.

The government has issued clear guidelines on the maximum daily alcohol intake for adults. The figures are two to three units a day for women, and three to four units a day for men, with alcohol-free days recommended for everyone. Women have a lower daily allowance than men because their bodies tend to be smaller and lighter and contain less water. Women also have smaller livers and metabolise alcohol more slowly. So, drink for drink, alcohol will usually have a more significant effect on a woman than on a man.

The good news is that drinking little and often can be positively good for your health. Studies show that men over 40 and women past the menopause who regularly drink one or two units of alcohol a day (not just red wine, as was previously thought) are less likely to develop coronary HEART DISEASE than non-drinkers.

On the down side, drinking more than the daily limits sets up a whole range of health hazards. Because it is high in calories, alcohol can contribute to obesity. Stouts and beer are the main culprits: although they contain fewer calories than either wine or spirits, they tend to be drunk in larger quantities. Most alcoholic drinks lack any essential vitamins and minerals. So drinking too much can provide lots of calories but still leave you short of vital nutrients needed for good health.

'Binge drinking' – random bouts of drinking to excess – has several harmful effects. Because alcohol affects your physical co-ordination and reaction times, such sessions put you and others at serious risk of accidents; they also take a heavy toll on your liver, making it less able to store fat-soluble vitamins and to metabolise protein. Binge drinking can also bring on attacks of GOUT or pancreatitis and even trigger abnormal heart rhythms.

It is now beyond doubt that excessive alcohol consumption damages long-term health. Alcohol raises your blood pressure. The more you drink, the more the pressure increases – and with it the chances of coronary heart disease and certain kinds of stroke. Regularly drinking too much leads to liver damage. One in five of all heavy drinkers develops cirrhosis of the liver, and one in five cirrhosis victims dies of liver

Treated with respect, alcohol can play a part in a healthy lifestyle. Moderation is the key and it is a good idea to make sure you have regular alcohol-free days.

cancer. Regular drinking is also linked with cancers of the mouth and the throat – and the risks are even higher among those who smoke as well.

About five in every 100 heavy drinkers suffer from alcoholism, an addictive – some say inherited – illness. As well as facing the health hazards of prolonged alcohol misuse, alcoholics often suffer from malnutrition, as they often neglect meals in favour of alcohol. Even for non-alcoholics there are times when just one drink can be too many – for example, when you are driving, operating machinery, or participating in active sports; or if you are taking certain medicines (check the label or ask your doctor if in doubt).

Because alcohol can both reduce the ability to conceive and adversely affect the baby in the womb, women who are trying to become pregnant or at any stage of PREGNANCY should either avoid drinking completely or aim to drink no more than one unit of alcohol a day.

alcohol measures

ONE UNIT = SINGLE MEASURE SPIRITS = SMALL GLASS SHERRY = SMALL GLASS WINE = ½ PINT BEER

	alcohol content by volume	units	maximum daily limits FOR MEN: 3–4 units	FOR WOMEN: 2–3 units	kcals
SPIRITS Standard bottle (750ml)	40%	30			
Single pub measure (50ml)		1	3–4 measures OR	2–3 measures OR	50 per measure
WINE Standard bottle (750ml)	8–14%	6–10½			
Single pub measure (125ml)		1–1½	2–3 measures OR	1–2 measures OR	85 per glass (sweet white 100)
ORDINARY BEER, LAGER OR CIDER Large can (440ml)	3.5%	1½	2 large cans OR	1–2 large cans OR	140
Small can (275ml)		1	3–4 small cans OR	2–3 small cans OR	90
1 pint		2	1½–2 pints	1–1½ pints	180 (sweet cider 220)

Use this chart to monitor your daily alcohol intake. It shows the maximum number of units that it is safe for men and women to drink in one day. However, government guidelines also recommend that everyone should aim to have one or two alcohol-free days every week.

More and more people think they are allergic to certain foods – but in fact they may have a food intolerance

allergies

All allergies are triggered by allergens – tiny particles of matter found in the environment or in food. In themselves these particles are harmless, but the body of someone who is susceptible to a particular allergen (or allergy) sees them as hostile invaders. It responds to their threat by releasing an army of antibodies that team up with cells lining the skin, nose, eyes, lips, mouth, lungs and intestines, prompting a sudden release of histamine. This gives rise to the classic symptoms of an allergy – anything from mild hay fever to the potentially fatal reactions triggered in people allergic to peanuts.

Common allergens include pollen, dust mites, animal hair, feathers, tobacco smoke, exhaust fumes, bee stings and some foods or food ingredients. The same allergen can provoke different reactions in different people, while similar symptoms can be triggered by different allergens. To complicate matters further, children and adults often outgrow allergies for no known reason. And a new allergy, particularly one triggered by food, can strike at any age.

Recent surveys show that at least two in every ten people in Britain believe they are allergic to certain foods. Yet government figures suggest only one person in 50 has a food allergy (rising to one in ten among those with a family history of allergy).

This indicates the tendency to confuse an allergy with an intolerance. The term food allergy applies only when the immune system over-reacts to a normally harmless food. Other adverse reactions to food (anything from a severe headache to wind) that do not involve the immune system are due to food intolerance.

No food is harmful in itself, but those that are known to trigger an allergy in susceptible people include milk, eggs, peanuts and other nuts, soya, fish and shellfish.

food note

The following foods seldom, if ever, set off adverse reactions:

1 **Peaches, apples and pears.**

2 **Carrots, lettuce and globe artichokes.**

3 **Rice – whether white, brown or wild.**

food note

Nuts – especially peanuts – milk, eggs, soya, fish and shellfish are all known to trigger allergic reactions in susceptible people.

Occasionally food ADDITIVES are culprits. Food allergens can cause ASTHMA, ECZEMA, nettle rash (HIVES) and a host of other problems, from a mild headache to a severe stomach upset. A specific food can trigger widely different responses in different people. A single peanut, for example, can bring on an attack of asthma – and in extreme cases prompt a histamine explosion throughout the whole body, causing a life-threatening anaphylaxis. (This is usually treated with an adrenaline injection.)

The only way to prevent a reaction is to avoid the offending food. To identify it, a skin or blood test may be suggested. Alternatively, your doctor or dietician might recommend an exclusion diet, in which suspect foods are systematically eliminated from your diet.

Food intolerances can sometimes be identified in this way, too. The most common food intolerance in the West is to cow's milk. This afflicts people who cannot produce lactase, an enzyme needed to digest milk. (Milk and eggs are also associated with childhood eczema.)

Wheat is another everyday food that can trigger adverse reactions. People with gluten intolerance (see COELIAC DISEASE) cannot absorb nutrients properly because gluten (found in cereals such as wheat and rye) damages the lining of their intestine.

John is a healthy eight-year-old who happens to have a peanut allergy. His parents are adept at screening peanuts out of his diet, but one day he touched an empty bag of peanuts and later put his hand to his mouth. Within two hours he was in Accident and Emergency, wheezing and with swollen, itchy eyes. His parents had already given him some antihistamine to reduce the allergic reaction; in hospital he was given an adrenaline injection and kept in for observation. John's parents now always carry an adrenaline injection Epipen, and John wears a wristband that warns of his allergy.

alzheimer's disease

This form of dementia tends mainly to strike elderly people; early symptoms include confusion and short-term memory lapses. But over time the person's mind may deteriorate to the point where he or she can no longer cope without help.

People with Alzheimer's tend to lack certain nutrients, so carers should provide nutritious meals that are easy to eat. There may be a link between aluminium and the development of the disease. So try not to use aluminium pans to cook acidic foods, such as tomatoes or rhubarb, which can dissolve aluminium. And avoid the food additive E541, a raising agent containing sodium aluminium phosphate, and antacid indigestion remedies high in aluminium hydroxide. Silicon prevents our bodies from absorbing aluminium and occurs naturally in cabbage, lettuce, alfalfa, green vegetables, onions, milk and beer – so the occasional pint may be helpful.

Vitamin E supplements may slow the progression of Alzheimer's, according to a recent study. Foods rich in vitamin E include wheatgerm, nuts and seeds.

eat more

Alfalfa, spinach and other leafy vegetables.

avoid

1 **Using aluminium pans to cook acidic foods.**

2 **Cakes, breads and pastries containing the food additive E541.**

3 **Indigestion tablets that contain aluminium compounds.**

anaemia

When the level of either red blood cells or haemoglobin in our blood is low, less oxygen reaches our body tissues and anaemia can result. The most common cause is iron deficiency, and those most at risk are teenage girls, women in their reproductive years, vegetarians and elderly people.

The richest food source of iron is liver; others include red meat, eggs, fresh green vegetables and fortified breakfast cereals. Our bodies absorb iron more readily from animal food sources than from plant foods but you can double your uptake from plant food if you eat a food rich in vitamin C at the same meal. On the other hand, tannin in tea and phytic acid in brown rice and wheat bran reduce iron absorption.

Anaemia is sometimes caused by a lack of folate or vitamin B_{12}. People on VEGETARIAN and vegan diets often lack vitamin B_{12} since it is not found in plant foods, and all women are at risk of folate deficiency, especially during pregnancy. Symptoms of anaemia include lethargy, dizziness, palpitations and swollen legs. See your doctor for specialist advice and treatment.

eat more

1 **Liver (unless you're pregnant) and red meat.**

2 **Fresh green leafy vegetables for folate.**

3 **Fortified breakfast cereals for iron.**

4 **Blackcurrants, citrus fruit, potatoes and red peppers for vitamin C.**

avoid

Drinking tea with meals: it can reduce iron uptake by 50 per cent.

antioxidants

sources

1 Brightly coloured fruit and vegetables, such as carrots, red peppers, tomatoes, apricots and mangoes for beta carotene. Other good sources are watercress and spinach.

2 Foods rich in vitamins C and E.

3 Wholegrain foods, nuts and shellfish for antioxidant minerals.

We need antioxidants, which are a group of naturally occurring chemicals, to help prevent ailments such as heart disease and strokes as well as some forms of cancer. Antioxidants help to control free radicals – molecules that fight off infections, but if left unchecked can cause cholesterol to deposit in the arteries, and can damage DNA (the genetic code carried in cells), which may trigger cancer.

It is now widely accepted that people who eat antioxidant-rich foods are less prone to these conditions. The main antioxidants found in food are vitamin E (in vegetable oils, margarine, nuts, avocados), vitamin C (in fruit and vegetables, such as citrus fruit, kiwi fruit, potatoes, green and red peppers), and beta carotene, the plant form of vitamin A (in carrots, spinach, apricots).

Some minerals are also important antioxidants: these are selenium (in shellfish, wholegrain cereals and Brazil nuts), copper (in shellfish, nuts and seeds) and zinc (in oysters and most shellfish). Flavonoids are another group of antioxidants found abundantly in most fruits and vegetables.

apples

benefits

1 Good source of vitamin C and – when unpeeled – fibre.

2 Stewed apples may help to stop diarrhoea.

The saying 'An apple a day keeps the doctor away' has led many people to believe that apples are a particularly healthy food. So what are their benefits?

Apples are a good source of vitamin C: cooking apples and Granny Smiths contain slightly more than sweeter varieties such as Cox and Golden Delicious. Unpeeled apples are also a useful source of fibre, and naturopaths often prescribe them to treat constipation. On the other hand, stewed apples are used to treat diarrhoea because of their pectin content, which helps liquid to gel. A typical eating apple contains about 50 Calories – mostly in the form of fructose, a natural sugar that supplies a slow, steady source of energy. Weight for weight, dried apples contain six times the calories of fresh ones, and although their vitamin C is lost in the drying process, they make a useful snack for athletes.

Apple juice is a good source of vitamin C but does not provide any fibre. Because of its high fructose content, it has almost as many calories as most sweet, fizzy drinks – about 80 Calories in an average glass.

apricots

Fresh apricots are one of the best natural sources of beta carotene – the plant form of vitamin A and an antioxidant that helps reduce the risk of heart disease and cancer. They are rich in potassium, which helps regulate blood pressure, and in soluble fibre, which helps to control blood sugar.

Although dried apricots contain far more calories than fresh, they still make a healthy snack. Drying them concentrates the levels of beta carotene, potassium and iron so that a handful of dried apricots, for example, provides about a fifth of the suggested daily intake of potassium for adults and almost 20 per cent of the iron intake suggested for men.

To preserve their colour, dried apricots are often treated with sulphur dioxide (E220), which can trigger an asthma attack in susceptible people. Unsulphured fruit looks less appealing and contains less beta carotene but is usually preservative-free. 'Ready-to-eat' dried apricots may contain more preservatives than fully dried fruit.

Apricots with the most intensely coloured orange flesh are the richest in beta carotene.

benefits

1 Rich source of beta carotene.

2 Dried apricots are an excellent source of potassium and a good source of iron.

3 High in soluble fibre.

drawback

Some dried apricots are treated with sulphur dioxide and should be avoided by people suffering from asthma.

food note

Apricot kernels contain a substance that can produce prussic acid and they are therefore toxic.

arthritis

eat more

1 Oil-rich fish, such as salmon, mackerel and sardines.

2 Fresh fruit and vegetables.

3 Wholemeal bread and wholegrain cereals.

4 Fresh ginger.

eat less

1 Refined foods.

2 Saturated fats.

3 Sugar and salt.

Osteoarthritis and rheumatoid arthritis are the two main types of this painful condition characterised by stiff and swollen joints. In osteoarthritis, joint cartilage gradually breaks down or hardens, causing bones to rub together and warp. In rheumatoid arthritis, the body's immune system turns on itself and attacks the joints.

Anyone with osteoarthritis should cut down on highly refined foods, saturated animal fats, sugar and salt, and eat more wholegrain cereals, vegetables and fresh fruit. A well-balanced, low-fat diet plus regular exercise – a daily ten-minute walk or swim – will help maintain muscle tone and reduce the risk of becoming overweight, which puts extra strain on joints.

There is scientific evidence that fish oils can help reduce inflammation; some studies have found that a vegetarian diet can also offer relief. An ALLERGY or a food intolerance can be a contributing factor: one way to find suspect foods is to follow an exclusion diet, but only under medical supervision. Finally, fresh ginger has also been shown to help arthritis sufferers.

asparagus

benefits

1 Diuretic effect.

2 Mild laxative.

3 Can help relieve indigestion.

4 Can act as a sedative.

drawback

Can aggravate gout by raising uric acid levels in the blood.

As well as being a delicacy, steamed tender asparagus spears are a useful source of folate and antioxidant vitamins (green spears contain slightly more beta carotene and vitamin C than white ones). Asparagus acts as a diuretic and can help relieve fluid retention. It is also a mild laxative. Herbalists use it to treat indigestion, and as a sedative for heart palpitations.

On the down side, the sulphur-producing chemicals in asparagus make urine smell. A high purine content in asparagus can also aggravate GOUT, by raising uric acid levels.

Asthma is an allergic condition that can be triggered by anything from stress to animal hair or certain foods

asthma

Asthma is a chronic, potentially serious respiratory condition that in rare cases can cause death. In the UK, one in every 25 adults has asthma, as do one in seven schoolchildren – though studies show that some children outgrow the disease by the time they reach adulthood.

Along with other allergic conditions such as ECZEMA and hay fever, asthma tends to run in families. Symptoms, which are caused by inflamed bronchial passages, include wheezing, shortness of breath and a tight chest. Common triggers include anxiety, stress, environmental pollution, pollen, dust mites and animal hair. Food allergies may also start off attacks or make them worse. Suspect foods include cow's milk, wheat and other cereals, yeast and food that contains mould, such as Stilton and other blue cheeses. Nuts (especially peanuts), fish and eggs can produce the most immediate and dangerous reactions.

Certain food additives may also prompt asthma attacks. Under EU legislation, every additive present in packaged food must be listed on the label, so check carefully if you know you are sensitive to them. Additives that may bring on an asthma

Anna is 18 and has suffered from asthma since birth. She also has mild eczema and is allergic to cats and aspirin. Her asthma grew progressively worse and she had been admitted to hospital several times by the time she was 14, at which point her GP sent her to an allergy clinic. Pinprick tests revealed that she is also allergic to dairy products, tomatoes and nuts. By cutting right down on these foods – but not avoiding them completely – her asthma has improved dramatically. Although Anna still uses an inhaler from time to time, she has not been readmitted to hospital.

eat more

1 **Foods rich in B vitamins, such as leafy green vegetables and pulses.**

2 **Good sources of magnesium – green vegetables, sunflower seeds and dried figs.**

avoid

Foods that you know are likely to trigger an asthma attack. These might be:

1 **Nuts (especially peanuts), fish and eggs.**

2 **Cow's milk and cereals.**

3 **Foods containing yeast or mould, such as bread and blue cheeses.**

4 **Foods containing additives such as benzoates (E210-19), sulphites (E220-28) or gallates (E310-12).**

5 **Cider, wine and beer.**

6 **Foods and drinks containing colourings E102, E104 and E110.**

food note

Naturopaths treat asthma with cooked onions, which act as a decongestant, and tea. Tea contains theophylline, a relative of caffeine, which can help to dilate the bronchial tubes and ease breathing.

attack include benzoate preservatives (E210-19), found in soft drinks, chewing gum, low-calorie jams and fish roe; antioxidant additives used in certain fats, oils and breakfast cereals, namely the gallates (E310-12), BHA or E320 and BHT or E321. Colourings may also trigger an asthma attack: check all food and drink labels for E102 (tartrazine), E104 (quinolene yellow) and E110 (sunset yellow).

Sulphites (E220-28), used to preserve dried fruit, jams, and processed or frozen vegetables, pose a risk to some asthmatics. Sulphites also occur in beers and wines (simply inhaling the bouquet can trigger attacks in the most sensitive people).

No special diet will help all asthma sufferers. However, those whose attacks result from stress may benefit from foods rich in B vitamins, especially B_6 (in meat and fish). Studies also show that magnesium, found in wholegrain cereals, pulses and dried figs, can help by relaxing the airways, and that oil-rich fish, a source of omega-3 fatty acids, may protect against asthma as it has an anti-inflammatory effect on the lungs.

avocados

benefits

1 Rich source of vitamin E.

2 Good source of potassium.

3 Contain high levels of monounsaturated fat.

drawback

High in calories.

Avocados are highly nutritious. Just one average-sized fruit can supply the adult daily requirement of vitamin E, an antioxidant that may protect against cancer.

Along with such foods as bananas, pulses and dried fruit, avocados are an especially good source of potassium, the mineral that plays a vital role in maintaining a regular heartbeat and controlling blood pressure, and without which nerves and muscles cannot function properly. They also contain useful amounts of vitamin B_6 – important for a healthy nervous system – as well as vitamin C, which helps to keep skin healthy. In addition, avocados contain more protein than any other fruit.

In common with olive oil, avocados have high levels of monounsaturated FATS. These can help to lower blood cholesterol levels – although they are not quite as effective as polyunsaturated fats.

The only drawback of avocados for some weight-conscious people is their very high calorie count. The flesh of one avocado contains up to 400 Calories – and that is before you add any dressing.

Avocados are a good source of potassium, the mineral that plays a vital role in maintaining a regular heartbeat and controlling blood pressure.

Introducing nutritious food to babies is a vital step that lays the foundation for a healthy life ahead

babies

Breast milk gives a baby the best possible start in life. It contains all the nutrients a baby needs in exactly the right proportions and is easy to digest. Even breast feeding for just the first few days ensures that important antibodies are passed from mother to baby. And breast feeding for at least four months, preferably six, reduces the risk of the baby developing allergies if there is a family history of allergy as well as conferring long-term health benefits.

Manufactured milk (or formula milk) is designed to supply a similar range of nutrients to breast milk, using modified cow's milk or soya milk as a base. The latter may be a better option if anyone in the family has had an allergy to cow's milk.

Breast milk or formula provides all your baby's nutritional needs for the first six months. Thereafter your baby will still need about a pint a day of breast milk or formula, up to one year of age. At six months, pasteurised cow's milk can be introduced into the diet, but only as part of a meal (on cereal or in sauces for example): it should not be your baby's main drink under 12 months as it has insufficient iron. So if you stop breast feeding before this age, give your baby a 'follow-on' formula milk until he or she is a year old.

Starting on solids

Most babies are ready to begin weaning from around four months old. Weaning before this age increases the risk of allergies later in life. The simplest way to start is by offering a teaspoon of puréed vegetable or fruit – with no added sugar or salt, of course. Do this for just one feed a day and be prepared for your baby to take some time to learn to eat from a spoon: until now, food has always come in a stream of liquid. Easy foods to try include puréed carrot, potato, apple, banana or specially manufactured baby rice. Start with just one food at a time and then gradually introduce other flavours. Two or three new foods a week is usually quite enough for a baby to cope with.

Because of possible allergic reactions, babies should not be given wheat-based foods, eggs, foods that contain traces of nuts, or citrus fruits until they are about six months old. Whole nuts should never be given to young children because of the risk of choking. If you suspect any tendency to allergy in your family, ask your health visitor for advice. Department of Health nutritional guidelines for feeding babies and young children are constantly reviewed and your health visitor is the best person to keep you up to date with current advice.

Introducing new foods

Continue to breast feed or bottle feed while weaning your baby, and gradually increase the number of feed times at which you offer solid food. At the same time, slowly increase the quantity of food given. Then you can start to introduce puréed foods that include meat, fish or pulses. As your baby gets older, foods can be mashed rather than puréed. And once babies have learned to hold objects, they can be given a peeled carrot or chunk of peeled apple to chew on, or a piece of crusty bread. Always stay close at hand in case of choking.

Ready-made, manufactured baby foods can be a real help when time is short or you are going out for the day, for example. Most common brands offer fruit or vegetable purées with no added sugar or salt; some top brands are prepared from organically grown ingredients. But ultimately, your aim is to help your baby enjoy eating the same food as the rest of the family. So gradually introduce a range of foods but avoid too much sugar and salt.

first foods

1 Start with vegetable and fruit purées. Try carrot, potato, banana or apple.

2 Manufactured baby rice is another good convenient option.

avoid

1 Giving babies wheat, cow's milk, eggs, finely ground nuts and citrus fruits until they are six months old, to reduce the risk of allergy.

2 Whole nuts, which should not be given to infants because of the risk of choking.

case study

Ben is five months old and has been breast feeding since birth. His mother, Mary, recognises that breast milk helps protect her baby against infections and lowers his risk of allergies. However, Ben suffered a nasty bout of colic shortly after he was born. Mary was advised by her GP to look to her diet for clues to the causes, as some babies react adversely to food their mother has eaten. The most common culprits are caffeine-containing drinks, alcohol, onions, garlic and citrus fruits. In Ben's case, orange juice was the problem. When Mary cut out her daily glass of juice, Ben's problem disappeared.

bad breath

eat more

Vegetables and fruit to avoid constipation.

avoid

Eating garlic, raw onions, curries and sugary foods, and drinking too much alcohol.

Bad breath that is simply the result of over-indulgence in alcohol, curry or dishes cooked with garlic can be camouflaged by chewing aromatic dill, caraway, cardamom or fennel seeds, which are often offered to diners at the end of a meal in curry restaurants. Parsley, too, is a traditional remedy to mask the smell of garlic on the breath.

Persistent bad breath (halitosis) can be due to a number of factors. A decaying tooth or gum infections are likely causes, but bad breath can also result from constipation, sinusitis, a chest infection or a stomach ulcer. Drinking an extra glass of water a day guards against constipation, particularly if you also eat more wholegrain cereals and fruit and vegetables.

Sometimes bad breath is associated with medical conditions such as diabetes, irritable bowel syndrome, and kidney or liver problems, and doctors are now starting to take diagnosis by breath more seriously. Research is well under way to develop a machine sensitive enough to detect minute traces of compounds in the breath that may indicate the presence of disease.

balancing your diet

eat more

1 Fruit and vegetables.

2 Bread, rice, pasta and potatoes.

3 Low-fat yogurts, milks and other dairy products.

eat less

1 Excessively fatty and sugary foods.

2 Salt and salty foods.

Government guidelines on nutrition can sometimes sound nannying and overly complicated, but they are in fact easy to follow and can form the basis for a healthy lifestyle. They are not a rigid set of daily rules, just an overall balance to aim for. Your diet is bound to be 'less healthy' on some days than others. This does not matter as long as you compensate for any 'lapses' over the next few days.

Foods are classified into five groups: fruit and vegetables; carbohydrates (bread, rice, pasta, potatoes); proteins (meat, fish, nuts, beans, eggs); milk and dairy products; and fatty and sugary foods. It can help to picture your ideal daily intake as a large plate of food, with carbohydrates covering a third of it, fruits and vegetables making up another third and the remaining food groups together comprising the last third (see the diagram opposite).

Nutritionists have measured out recommended daily intakes of calories, fats, sugars and salt that will keep people of average build and weight in good health. Calories measure the amount of energy a

how to size up your diet

For a balanced diet rich in all the vital nutrients, choose your foods in the proportions shown on this 'plate'. If you don't manage to achieve these ratios every day, aim for an overall balance over a period of a week or so.

Bread, pasta, rice, cereals and potatoes

These foods are our main source of the starchy carbohydrates and nutritionists urge us to eat more of them, in preference to higher-fat foods.

Fruit and vegetables

Choose a wide variety of foods in this group, to ensure you are getting all the essential vitamins and minerals. You can use them as snacks, side and main dishes, in sauces, and in drinks and desserts.

Milk and dairy

These foods should be eaten in moderation. Reduced-fat varieties – such as half-fat milk or yogurt – are the healthiest options for adults.

Fatty and sugary foods

Foods such as butter, margarine, oils, crisps, chocolate and ice cream can form part of a healthy diet as long as they are eaten in moderation.

Meat and fish

Eat modest amounts of meat – opting for leaner cuts where possible. Try to include fish in your diet (especially oil-rich varieties) at least twice a week.

food groups

The nutrients in each food group

CARBOHYDRATES
BREAD, CEREALS (RICE, OATS, WHEAT), PASTA, POTATOES

Starch for energy.
Calcium for strong teeth and bones.
Magnesium for healthy bones, teeth, nerves and muscles.
Iron to guard against anaemia.
B vitamins for releasing energy from food.
Fibre (in wholemeal bread, brown rice, potatoes and some cereals) for helping to prevent constipation and to lower blood cholesterol levels.

FRUIT AND VEGETABLES
(EXCLUDING POTATOES)

A range of vitamins and minerals.
Carotenes for antioxidant protection and healthy eyesight.
Folates for cell division and to guard against some birth defects.
Fibre for preventing constipation and to lower blood cholesterol levels.
Carbohydrates for energy.

MILK AND DAIRY PRODUCTS
(EXCLUDING BUTTER AND CREAM)

Calcium for healthy teeth and bones.
Protein for growth and repair.
Riboflavin to release energy from food.
Vitamin A for growth and cell development, and healthy eyesight.
Vitamin B_{12} for making DNA and RNA, and for nerve cell activity.

PROTEINS
MEAT, FISH, BEANS, EGGS, NUTS

Protein for growth and repair.
Iron to guard against anaemia.
Zinc for growth and reproduction.
B vitamins to release energy from food.

FATTY AND SUGARY FOODS
BUTTER, MARGARINE, COOKING OILS; SWEETS, CAKES AND BISCUITS

Fatty foods provide:
Essential fatty acids for growth and healthy skin.
Vitamin E to protect from free-radical damage.
Also help the body to absorb vitamin A (for eyesight); vitamins E and D (for healthy bones and teeth); vitamin K (for normal blood clotting).

Most sugary foods contain few useful nutrients.

diet supplies. In general, men need about 2,500 Calories a day and women slightly less – around 2,000. But lifestyle, age, and your metabolic rate also affect your precise needs. For total fats in the diet, the recommended amounts are 95g for men and 70g for women. Sugars are slightly lower – 70g and 50g respectively – and neither men nor women need more than a teaspoon of salt a day. So it is wise not to sprinkle salt all over your meals, as many foods contain hidden salt that contributes to your permitted daily teaspoonful.

As well as fats, carbohydrates and proteins, our bodies need several vitamins and minerals to function properly. No one food can provide all these nutrients. Eating a varied diet is the best way to ensure you get a good supply of them all. By doing so, you should not need vitamin and mineral supplements, except in special circumstances. For example, doctors may prescribe folic acid and iron to women trying to conceive or in the early stages of pregnancy. Vitamin B_{12} is sometimes recommended for people suffering from some forms of ANAEMIA.

How you prepare and cook your food can significantly affect its nutritional value. As a general rule, grilling is healthier than frying, and steaming is preferable to boiling.

A nourishing anywhere, anytime snack – conveniently packaged by nature

bananas

Bananas are rich in potassium – a mineral that is vital to our health. Potassium works in tandem with another mineral, sodium, to control the body's fluid balance and heartbeat, as well as its nerve and muscle functions. An excess of one mineral will suppress the action of the other. And since most of us have too much sodium in our diet (thanks to our liberal intake of salt), extra potassium is often beneficial.

As bananas contain readily absorbed simple carbohydrates, they provide an almost immediate supply of energy, which makes them a popular snack for athletes (especially tennis players), before or during a competition.

Ripe bananas are easy to digest, and seldom trigger allergic reactions, making them an invaluable first food for weaning babies. They are also ideal for anyone who is recovering from an upset stomach. The starch in unripe bananas is much less digestible, however, and is known as resistant starch – it can ferment in the large intestine and cause wind. Green bananas (plantains) are high in resistant starch because they are eaten before they are ripe. They are indigestible and unpalatable unless they are cooked. Some research has suggested a link between diets that are high in resistant starch and a reduced risk of both stomach and bowel cancer. Scientists are still investigating this possibility.

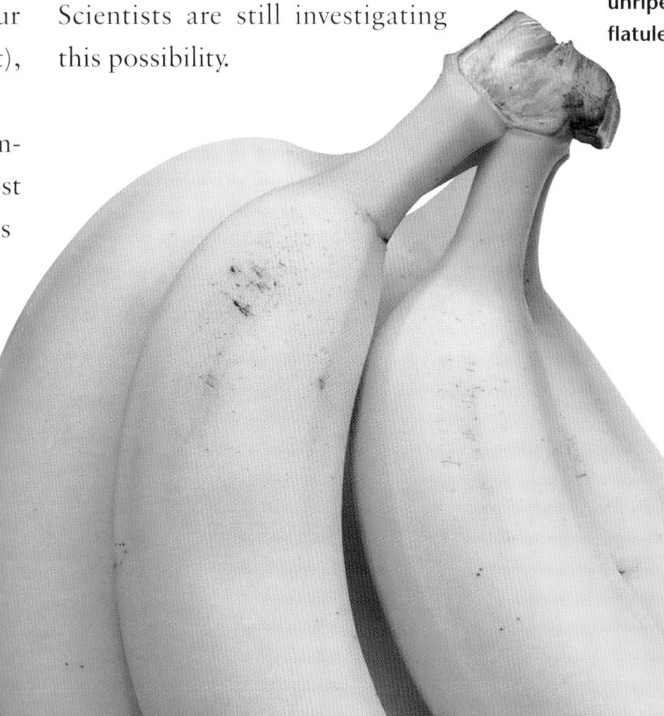

benefits

1 High in potassium.

2 Easily digested when ripe for quick energy release.

drawback

Resistant starch in unripe fruit can cause flatulence.

Broad beans are more nutritious than French or runner beans, but all three supply useful amounts of fibre

beans

benefits

1 Supply protein and soluble fibre.

2 Low in calories.

3 Provide beta carotene, which the body converts to vitamin A.

drawbacks

1 Broad beans may react with certain antidepressant drugs to produce high blood pressure.

2 Broad beans can trigger anaemia in susceptible people.

All beans belong to the legume family of vegetables. Broad beans, green or French beans and runner beans are discussed here. For bean sprouts and beans and pulses that are normally sold dried or in cans – such as lentils, kidney beans, soya beans and baked (haricot) beans – see PULSES.

Green beans are low in calories and provide a useful source of protein. They supply soluble fibre, which can help to protect against bowel problems and may help to lower blood cholesterol levels. They also contain minerals such as potassium and vitamins C, E and beta carotene (which the body converts into vitamin A) and niacin.

Nutritionally, broad beans win out over green, French or runner beans. Weight for weight, broad beans contain significantly more protein, calories, starch and fibre than green or French beans (which in turn contain more than runner beans). Broad beans also provide more potassium for healthy blood pressure, phosphorus and calcium for strong teeth and bones, iron to protect against ANAEMIA and beta carotene for healthy skin and eyes.

All of these beans are widely available frozen. Freezing does not greatly affect their nutrient value, but canning destroys significant amounts of their vitamin C.

Broad beans contain a substance called vicine, which can trigger a severe anaemic reaction – known as favism – in certain people of Mediterranean origin. Broad beans are also incompatible with some types of drugs. Anyone taking any of a group of antidepressants known as monoamine oxidase inhibitors (MAOIs) should exclude broad beans from their diet as the combination of broad beans and these drugs can produce an abrupt surge in blood pressure.

beetroot

This staple of summer salads is one of the few vegetables that retain their nutrient and vitamin content after boiling. Beetroot is a good source of folate – needed during the early stages of pregnancy to reduce risks of spina bifida. It is rich in potassium, a mineral vital for maintaining the body's fluid balance and blood pressure, and for regulating heartbeat, nerve and muscle function. It also contains vitamin C. The pigment that gives beetroot its characteristic colour is used in the food industry to make ice cream, soups and even burgers look more appetising. After eating it our urine and stools can turn pink, because our bodies cannot metabolise it.

If you grow your own beetroot, do not discard the leafy tops. They can be cooked and served like spinach, and contain useful amounts of beta carotene (the vegetable form of vitamin A), calcium and iron.

benefits

1 Rich in potassium.

2 A source of folate.

3 Can be boiled with little loss of nutrients.

avoid

Pickling beetroot in vinegar, as this reduces the level of nutrients.

biscuits, cakes and pastries

Biscuits, cakes and pastries are treats that we all enjoy, but they do not offer significant amounts of nutrients. They all rely on a high-calorie combination of sugar and fats. All three tend to be made from solid fats high in saturated fats, which have been linked to coronary heart disease.

Homemade versions of cakes, biscuits and pastries can be made to more healthy recipes. Cakes, for example, can be made with extra dried fruit or grated carrot that makes the cake moist so the fat content can be reduced. Biscuits can be baked with bran or oats to increase their nutritional value. But on the whole it is not worth the effort to try to make a cake that is actually 'good' for you: instead, treat yourself once in a while. Reduced-fat cakes and biscuits can still be deceptively high in sugar, and therefore in calories. Eating too many sweet biscuits of any kind can also contribute to tooth decay.

Biscuits with the lowest calorie counts include crackers and crispbreads, but do not be tempted to spread them with butter as their calorie value will soar.

food note

Biscuits, cakes and pastries are made from high-calorie combinations of fats and sugar. Try to limit your intake, but there is no need to cut them out of your diet altogether.

blackberries

benefits

1 Contain vitamin C.

2 A rich source of anthocyanins, thought to have antibacterial properties.

3 Contain some fibre and folate.

Juicy, ripe blackberries contain reasonable amounts of vitamin C, vital for healthy skin, teeth and gums and for fighting off infections. An average 100g (3½oz) serving contains 15mg. They are usually sweet enough to eat raw, particularly the cultivated varieties. Prolonged cooking reduces the vitamin C content, and adding large amounts of sugar, as in jam making, contributes unnecessary calories.

Blackberries' deep-purply-black colour is an indication of the presence of anthocyanins – flavonoids that are currently the subject of scientific research to determine their benefits, especially for the health of the eyes and in combating the food-poisoning bacteria *E. coli*. Blackberries also contain salicylate, which can provoke an asthma attack or hyperactivity in anyone sensitive to aspirin.

If picking wild blackberries from the hedgerows, avoid those growing on roadside verges, which may have high lead levels from traffic fumes. Similarly, those next to fields under cultivation may have been inadvertently sprayed with pesticides.

blackcurrants

benefits

1 Rich in vitamin C.

2 Anthocyanins in blackcurrant skins may have antibacterial and anti-inflammatory action.

Raw blackcurrants are one of the richest sources of vitamin C. Just 15g (½oz), barely a tablespoon, supplies 75 per cent of our suggested daily intake. The drawback is their short season, although they do freeze well, with relatively low loss of nutrients. Canned blackcurrants are not so nutritious, because of their reduced vitamin C content. As with blackberries, their colour indicates the presence of anthocyanins, and there is some evidence that those in blackcurrants play a role in inhibiting food-poisoning bacteria such as *E. coli*.

High blood pressure is a killer condition that has no obvious symptoms but can be controlled by diet

blood pressure

Typically, high blood pressure – or hypertension – occurs in middle age and affects one in seven people. Small blood vessels begin to lose elasticity in their muscular walls so that the heart encounters resistance when pumping blood round the body and has to work even harder to do so. Having high blood pressure increases the risks of suffering a stroke, or of damage to eyesight, because of the possibility of rupturing small blood vessels. It can also lead to kidney failure. A doctor will often prescribe drugs on initial diagnosis but, depending on the severity of the disease, it may be possible to control it by changes in diet and lifestyle alone once the drugs have done their job. At any rate, taking the following steps will help any drugs prescribed to work more efficiently.

Reducing your salt intake is crucial: excessive salt is associated with increased blood pressure. Do not add salt when cooking or to food at the table and cut right down on pickled, smoked and salted products. Giving up alcohol has a measurable long-term effect on lowering blood pressure and your doctor may suggest taking gentle exercise, such as a daily walk.

eat more

1 Fresh fruit and vegetables.

cut down on

1 Salt and salty foods. Your tastebuds will soon learn to adapt to a lower salt intake.

2 All smoked and pickled foods.

drink less

Alcohol.

case study

At 45, Kevin was diagnosed with hypertension or high blood pressure. His GP discussed ways by which he could change his lifestyle and help his condition. As he was slightly overweight he was advised to avoid fatty foods and increase his fibre intake. He also cut down on alcohol, smoking and salt. Kevin was surprised to find that many processed foods, even most breakfast cereals, have a hidden salt content. His blood pressure was checked monthly at first but as his diet and lifestyle improved the pressure fell and he needed only six-monthly checks. He says he feels much fitter now.

blood sugar levels

eat more

1 High-fibre snacks, such as vegetables, fruit, dried fruits, nuts and muesli.

2 Peas, beans, oats and other foods that contain slowly digested resistant starch.

cut down on

Sugary snacks such as sweets, biscuits and cakes. Eat them only in small amounts and at well-spaced intervals.

Why, shortly after eating a sugary snack, do you feel just as hungry as before? It is all down to the level of sugar in your blood. Sugar – specifically glucose – is the body's main source of fuel or energy, delivered via the bloodstream. The quantity in the blood at any one time is mainly regulated by a hormone called insulin. When you eat a sugary snack, glucose is quickly absorbed into the bloodstream, and the increased level prompts the pancreas to secrete extra insulin to 'mop up' the glucose and store it in the muscles and liver for future use. But if sugar levels are high, the pancreas can overreact and secrete too much insulin, and cause blood sugar levels to drop lower than they were before you ate. This is known as backlash hunger or the sugar trap. High-fibre foods and those with resistant starch (peas, beans and oats) release glucose more slowly, so there is less risk of being caught in the sugar trap. Slowly digested foods also help people who sometimes feel very tired and hungry and may faint if their blood sugar is low – a condition known as hypoglycaemia. (See also DIABETES.)

blueberries

benefit

Blueberries' antibacterial properties can soothe an upset stomach or cystitis.

drawback

Blueberries can cause an allergic reaction in those sensitive to berry fruits.

Blueberries have long been a traditional remedy for diarrhoea, and now folklore has been verified by science. Researchers have discovered that the berries contain anthocyanins, antibacterial compounds known to be effective against *E. coli* (the source of many gastric disorders). They are also recognised for their usefulness in preventing cystitis, which is often caused by *E. coli* in the urinary tract. And they have yet another weapon against bladder infection: blueberries (like cranberries) contain a compound that can prevent undesirable bacteria from attaching themselves to the mucous membranes of the bladder and urethra. Finally, blueberries – sweet enough to eat raw – are a good source of vitamin C, provided you eat a generous bowlful.

Bread – white or brown – is an extremely nutritious food yet most people do not eat enough

bread

Across much of the world, bread forms part of the daily diet. In the UK we eat an average of three slices a day, though many nutritionists would like to see that amount increased to at least five.

Once regarded as stodgy, fattening and a poor food source, bread is now valued for its complex carbohydrate content, which research has indicated helps to lower cholesterol levels in the blood. Wholemeal bread is also an excellent source of fibre, which can prevent digestive problems and may guard against some types of cancer. It is rich in iron and vitamins, too – particularly the B-complex group.

Even white bread is no longer scorned by nutritionists: these days it is made from flour fortified with added vitamins and minerals, including calcium for healthy teeth and bones. In fact, it is higher in calcium than wholemeal bread. It does not, however, contain as much fibre.

Traditionally, bread is made from flour, yeast and water (or milk). But as few of us can spare the time to make and bake our own nowadays, we rely on manufactured loaves. These usually contain added salt, a

eat more

1 **White, brown or wholemeal bread: it is an excellent source of valuable nutrients.**

2 **Wholemeal bread if you want to increase your fibre intake.**

eat less

Exotic breads such as croissants, brioche and naan. They tend to be higher in fat and sugar.

avoid

All bread if you are sensitive to gluten.

little fat, preservatives and emulsifiers. No matter what the ingredients, the process by which bread is formed remains the same: when flour is kneaded with water, the gluten proteins in the wheat soak up the liquid to make a dough; this traps gas bubbles from the fermenting yeast, which gives bread its texture. Breads made from 'strong' flour, with a high gluten content, have the lightest texture. Those made from 'soft' flours – such as rye – are lower in gluten and are denser. Sufferers of COELIAC DISEASE are intolerant to gluten and must avoid bread altogether, as it prevents their body from digesting other food properly. Supermarkets these days stock a diverse range of international breads. These include Italian ciabatta and focaccia, Eastern European and Jewish bagels, Scandinavian rye breads, Mexican tortillas, and Middle Eastern pittas. With such a varied choice widely available in our shops, it is easy to increase your daily intake of bread without ever becoming bored of it.

Bagels, the chewy Eastern European and Jewish rolls, are made from either white or wholemeal flour.

what's in bread?

The vital nutrients contained in bread

WHITE BREAD
MADE FROM REFINED FLOUR – MAY BE BLEACHED

Fortified with:
Calcium for healthy teeth and bones.
Thiamin for releasing energy from food.
Niacin for cell energy.
Iron to guard against anaemia.

WHOLEMEAL OR WHOLEWHEAT BREAD
MADE FROM WHOLEGRAIN FLOUR OR FROM WHITE FLOUR WITH ADDED BRAN AND WHEATGERM

Iron to guard against anaemia.
Zinc for normal growth and reproduction.
Phosphorus for strong bones and teeth.
Magnesium to maintain healthy bones, teeth, nerves and muscles.
Manganese for enzymes vital in energy production.
B vitamins to release energy from food.
Vitamin E to protect against free radicals.

BROWN
MADE FROM WHEAT FLOUR BUT WITH SOME BRAN REMOVED. CARAMEL IS SOMETIMES ADDED TO BOOST THE BROWN COLOUR.

Calcium for healthy teeth and bones.
Iron to guard against anaemia.
Zinc for normal growth and reproduction.
Phosphorus for healthy bones and teeth.
Magnesium for bones, teeth, nerves and muscles.
Manganese for enzymes in energy production.
B vitamins to release energy from food.

Levels of all nutrients, apart from calcium, are slighter lower than in wholemeal bread.

A generous helping of nutritious cereal in the morning can sustain you for several hours.

breakfast cereals

The only thing many of us have to eat in the morning is a hasty bowl of cereal. So it pays to make sure you are eating one of the more nutritious varieties. Porridge oats, for example, have been served at breakfast since Roman times and make a great start to the day. They are high in complex carbohydrates, which release energy gradually over several hours. Oats are also rich in soluble and insoluble fibre: the former helps reduce blood cholesterol levels; the latter can prevent constipation.

Oats make up a good proportion of the mix of cereals in muesli, which typically also contains dried fruits, wheat flakes and nuts. Wheat bran – the husks of wheat grains – is a source of insoluble fibre and the basis of high-fibre breakfast cereals, which usually feature the word bran somewhere in their brand name. Eating processed bran cereals is the best way to incorporate bran in your diet. However, check the packet, as liberal amounts of sugar and salt may have been added to improve the taste. Do not be tempted to sprinkle raw bran on your cereal: it is hard to swallow and may irritate the bowel.

Cereals for children are often fortified with vitamins and minerals, and offer a good source of energy. However, they tend to contain extra sugar to please young palates, so check the packet before you buy. Never give children extra high-fibre cereals: they can lead to digestive problems.

eat more

1 Oats for soluble and insoluble fibre, to help lower blood cholesterol and to prevent constipation.

2 Bran-based cereals, as another excellent source of insoluble fibre.

avoid

1 Adding raw bran to other cereals.

2 Giving young children breakfast cereals that are high in sugar, salt or fibre.

broccoli

benefits

1 A serving supplies the adult daily requirement of vitamin C, as well as useful amounts of beta carotene, folate, iron and potassium.

2 May help to protect against some forms of cancer.

For decades children have been urged to eat their greens – and no wonder when you consider broccoli. It is an excellent source of vitamin C and also contains beta carotene, which the body converts into vitamin A as it is needed, together with folate, iron and potassium.

Boosting folate levels before conception, and in the early stages of pregnancy, can reduce the risks of spina bifida in an unborn baby. A large 175g (6oz) serving of broccoli contains about a quarter of the recommended daily intake for the first 12 weeks of pregnancy. Like many members of the cabbage family, broccoli also contains certain phytochemicals that have been the focus of recent scientific interest. Research suggests that these compounds may offer protection against CANCER.

The darker the broccoli florets – whether they are purple, blue-green or deep green – the more useful nutrients they contain. Remember, however, that boiling your broccoli will halve the vitamin C content. Steaming, stir-frying and microwaving lead to a much smaller loss of the vitamin.

brussels sprouts

benefits

1 Rich in vitamin C for healthy skin, bones and teeth and essential for the absorption of iron.

2 May protect against some cancers, particularly those of the breast and uterus.

drawback

Like other members of the cabbage family, Brussels sprouts are well known for causing wind.

Brussels sprouts belong to the cabbage family and, like other vegetables in this group, contain chemical compounds that may protect the body from some cancers. In Brussels sprouts, these compounds are thought to be effective against cancers that are linked with increased levels of the hormone oestrogen in the body, such as breast and uterine cancers. It appears that the compounds may stimulate the liver to break down the excess oestrogen before it can do any damage to the body. Brussels sprouts are also a good source of folate, an increase in which is recommended for women trying to conceive or in the early stages of pregnancy, to guard against spina bifida. Like broccoli and other cruciferous vegetables, Brussels sprouts also supply vitamin C and beta carotene.

As with nearly all vegetables, cooking can have a drastic effect on the nutrient content of Brussels sprouts. If you prefer to boil Brussels sprouts, try not to over-boil them if you want to preserve their nutritional assets. Boil quickly, or slice and then steam. Alternatively, try stir-frying them.

Broccoli, a member of the cabbage family, is one of the most nutritious of vegetables – a source of vitamin C, beta carotene, folate, iron and potassium.

butter and margarine

benefits

Margarine and butter are good sources of vitamin A for healthy skin and eyesight, plus vitamin D for strong teeth and bones.

drawback

Eating too much butter or solid margarine could increase your risk of coronary heart disease, as both are high in saturated fats.

Whether you choose to put margarine or butter on your bread is ultimately a matter of taste. Margarine became increasingly popular after high-fat dairy foods were blamed for raising blood cholesterol levels. But in the backlash against over-processed foods, butter is gaining ground again.

Butter is a good source of vitamin A, needed for healthy eyesight, and vitamin D, without which we cannot absorb calcium for strong bones. Both vitamins are added to margarine by law. Margarine is made from vegetable oils, or a combination of these with fish oils or animal fats, colouring and flavourings. The oils in margarine are solidified by a process called hydrogenation, in which some of the unsaturated fats are turned into potentially unhealthy fats, called trans fats. Some manufacturers now sell products with a lower trans fat content.

Low-fat spreads are made mostly from water whipped up with butter or vegetable oils. Their levels of saturated fat vary quite a bit, so always check the label. New spreads are now available that actually claim to help reduce cholesterol levels.

cabbage

benefits

1 May help to prevent cancer of the colon.

2 May help to relieve peptic ulcers.

3 Excellent source of vitamin C.

drawback

May cause flatulence.

All types of cabbage are vitamin rich. The green varieties contain abundant vitamin C and K, and are a good source of vitamin E and potassium. They also supply beta carotene, folate, thiamin and fibre. Most nutrients are in the outer leaves.

Along with other cruciferous vegetables, cabbage contains compounds that may protect against certain cancers. Recent studies suggest that eating cabbage twice a week can lower the risk of colon cancer. Raw cabbage juice – about a litre (1¾ pints) a day for a week – is a traditional remedy for gastric ULCERS, but its effectiveness has yet to be scientifically proven. However, cabbage is notorious for causing flatulence – try cooking it with caraway or fennel seeds to combat this effect.

Adopting a healthy diet may significantly reduce your risk of developing certain types of cancer

cancer

According to the latest estimates, 35 per cent of cancers may be preventable by a long-term change in eating habits. This makes diet one of the single most important factors in causing cancer (smoking accounts for 30 per cent).

One in four people in this country dies of cancer, a disease in which the genetic material in cells is damaged so that they stop functioning normally. Instead, they proliferate at random, invading and destroying healthy tissue as they develop into abnormal growths. Lung cancer is the most common form in the UK. Next come cancers of the breast, bowel, prostate, bladder and stomach – all of which have dietary links.

To reduce the risk of cancer, eat plenty of fruit and vegetables, especially those high in vitamins A (beta carotene), C and E. These ANTIOXIDANTS can counteract the effects of free radicals, which are unstable molecules that may damage cells and trigger cancer. The fibre in fruit and vegetables, along with that in foods such as bread and cereals, is also useful. It can help to transport any toxins and carcinogens (cancer-forming substances) out of the body. And in any case, a diet lacking in essential nutrients weakens the immune system so it is less able to fight cancer cells.

Diet also influences levels of hormones in the body, which can affect a cancer's rate of growth. Indoles – nitrogen compounds found in broccoli, cabbage and Brussels sprouts – may protect against breast cancer by making oestrogen less potent.

With a high-fat diet you tend to put on excess weight, which is linked with cancer of the breast, womb and gall bladder. Fats should make up only about one-third of your daily calories. Higher intakes, particularly of saturated fats from animal sources, make the liver produce more bile, which in turn prompts bacteria in the gut to release potential carcinogens. Meat-eaters are more likely than vegetarians to suffer from colon cancer.

Eating a lot of grilled or barbecued food can be risky if it is charred – the burnt bits may contain carcinogens. Drinking excess alcohol has been linked to low blood levels of vitamins C and B, and to cancers of the mouth, oesophagus, larynx and liver.

eat more

1 **Fresh fruit and vegetables.**

2 **Wholegrain bread and cereals.**

eat less

1 **Fat, particularly saturated fat.**

2 **Red meat and processed meats.**

3 **Barbecued food if it is charred.**

drink less

Alcohol, which has been linked to cancers of the mouth, oesophagus, larynx and liver.

Once considered stodgy and fattening, bread, cereals and potatoes are now seen as key elements in a healthy diet

carbohydrates

eat more

Complex carbohydrates, such as bread, cereals, pasta and rice.

cut down on

Simple carbohydrates, contained in cakes, biscuits and sweets.

food note

One gram of carbohydrate (in the form of sugar or starch) supplies 4 Calories, much less than fat, which provides 9.

Most of our energy should be derived from carbohydrates, which come in three forms: sugars (simple carbohydrates), starch and fibre (both complex carbohydrates). These are present in varying amounts in different foods. The carbohydrate in a banana, for example, is mainly sugar, while in bread it is mostly starch. Carbohydrates are converted into glucose and glycogen, which supply fuel for the body. Simple sugars are absorbed quickly, providing a fast energy fix, while complex carbohydrates are broken down more slowly, for a sustained source of energy.

Grains, in the form of bread, rice and pasta, and vegetables such as potatoes and pulses, are our principal source of complex carbohydrates. They also supply protein, vitamins, minerals and fibre, with little fat. In the UK today, experts advise us to eat more of them, and reduce our fat intake accordingly. Government guidelines recommend that around half of our total daily calorie intake – about 1,000 Calories – should come from carbohydrates. An easy, healthy way to achieve this might be two slices of bread, a 225g (8oz) jacket potato, a portion of pasta, a digestive biscuit, a banana, an apple and an orange.

Starchy carbohydrates are dietary staples worldwide. Studies show that communities in the Western world with a low consumption of these foods tend to have higher rates of heart disease, strokes, obesity, cancer and bowel disorders. This could be because people who eat more starchy foods generally eat less fat, but starchy foods also supply fibre, which is now thought to protect against certain cancers.

A complex carbohydrate, pasta is a low-calorie food, if served with a plain tomato sauce.

carrots

Carrots are the richest common source of beta carotene, which our bodies convert to vitamin A. Unlike most vegetables, carrots are more nutritious cooked than raw. This is because cooking breaks down the cell membranes in the carrots, so the body can absorb twice as much carotene. It is true that carrots may help some people to see better in the dark. Good night vision depends on vitamin A combining with a protein present in the eye's retina. If you are deficient in vitamin A, your eyes may find it hard to adjust to dim light: eating a carrot a day should help. Larger carrots contain more carotene than baby ones.

Research shows that people with a high beta carotene intake from carrots and other vegetables are less likely to get certain cancers. There is evidence that eating raw carrots can reduce blood cholesterol levels. Always peel non-organic carrots before eating, and cut them well below the top, to remove any pesticide residues.

benefits

1 **Excellent source of beta carotene, the plant form of vitamin A.**

2 **May help protect against cancer.**

3 **Can help to lower blood cholesterol.**

cauliflower

Especially rich in vitamin C, cauliflower can provide more than the recommended daily intake in a single 100g (3½oz) portion when served raw. Although cooking does destroy some vitamin C, a lightly boiled portion of cauliflower still provides half the daily requirement. And at only 28 Calories per serving, cauliflower is an excellent choice for slimmers.

Like other members of the cruciferous family, such as broccoli, cauliflower contains phytochemicals that are thought to ward off some cancers, particularly of the colon. But cauliflower has a drawback, shared with other fibrous vegetables: it can cause flatulence as the gut breaks down the fibre. Cooking it with coriander, cumin, caraway or fennel may help the digestive process and reduce the problem.

Because it contains sulphur, cauliflower can sometimes give off an unpleasant smell during cooking, and by covering the pan, you risk the sulphur spoiling the flavour of the vegetable. It is usually better to use an open pan, and switch on the extractor fan or open a window.

benefits

1 **Good source of vitamin C.**

2 **May help to protect against certain cancers.**

drawback

May cause flatulence.

celery

benefits

1 May help to regulate blood pressure and keep the kidneys functioning efficiently.

2 May help to relieve gout.

3 Low in calories.

drawback

May be high in nitrates from fertilisers, unless organically grown.

An average-sized stick of celery contains a mere 4 Calories so it is very popular with slimmers. It is also a good source of potassium, which works with sodium to regulate the body's fluid levels. So celery (without salt) helps to maintain healthy blood pressure and to keep the kidneys functioning efficiently (by stimulating urine production to eliminate the body's waste products).

Celery also contains a mild, but valuable, anti-inflammatory agent. This can relieve painful joint conditions such as GOUT, caused by uric acid crystals forming in the joints. Herbalists often recommend tea made from celery seeds to gout sufferers. Another traditional use of celery is as a remedy for nervousness and hypertension. Naturopaths believe that celery seeds contain an oil that is thought to have a tranquillising effect.

Occasionally celery can be prone to high levels of nitrates from fertilisers. These can be harmful, especially to small children, so it is best not to eat large amounts of celery too regularly. Boiling or steaming helps to reduce nitrate levels.

cheese

benefits

1 Rich in both protein and calcium.

2 Important source of vitamin B_{12} for vegetarians.

drawbacks

1 Hard cheeses can be high in saturated fats, calories and salt.

2 May trigger migraines.

3 Risk of listeria bacteria in some unpasteurised cheeses.

Hard varieties of cheese such as Cheddar, Gloucester, Leicester and Parmesan are a good source of protein and rich in easily absorbed calcium (essential for strong bones). They also supply zinc, vitamin B_2 and vitamin B_{12} (particularly important in a vegetarian diet).

However, hard cheese tends to be the highest in saturated fats, which increase blood cholesterol levels and can lead to heart problems. Cheddar and Stilton contain about 35 per cent fat; soft cheeses such as Brie and Camembert contain about 26 per cent. Both ricotta and cottage cheese contain much less (around 11 and 4 per cent) and many different types of cheese are now available in low-fat versions, too.

A little-known fact is that cheese can help fight tooth decay. Tests show that eating small amounts after a meal can halve the number of cavities caused by sugar.

Cheese can aggravate disorders such as ECZEMA and migraine. Also, eating cheese made from unpasteurised milk can result in food poisoning, and so the elderly, invalids and pregnant women should avoid it.

Cherries are packed with potassium, which can help to offset the effects of excess sodium intake, such as fluid retention.

cherries

Plump, ripe cherries are a good source of potassium, which helps to regulate blood pressure. They also contain vitamin C.

There are more than 1,000 varieties of edible cherries, some sweet for eating raw, some sour for use in jams, pies and liqueurs. They range in colour from pale yellow to almost black. The deep pigments indicate the presence of anthocyanins, also found in fruits such as blackcurrants and bilberries. The compound is thought to protect against *E. coli*, a cause of bowel upsets and bladder infections. And cherries are credited with another therapeutic benefit: in traditional medicine they are valued for their reputed cleansing properties (helping to speed up the excretion of toxins from the body) thanks to their mild laxative effects. A tea made from cherry stalks is used as a traditional diuretic.

Cherries may also help people who suffer from GOUT, a painful swelling in the joints caused by a build-up of too much uric acid. Some experts believe that eating about 20 red or black cherries a day can lower uric acid levels and so offer some relief.

benefits

1 **Good source of potassium.**

2 **May help to alleviate symptoms of gout.**

3 **Laxative effects may relieve constipation.**

Poultry is a good source of protein, vitamins and minerals and a healthy choice for those on low-fat diets

chicken and poultry

benefits

1 Rich in most of the essential B vitamins.

2 Good source of protein and minerals.

3 Chicken and turkey livers supply generous amounts of vitamin A.

drawback

Poultry skin is relatively high in fat.

health tip

Chicken carries salmonella bacteria, which may cause food poisoning if chicken is undercooked. Salmonella survives freezing but is completely destroyed by thorough cooking.

Poultry includes farm-reared turkey, duck and goose, but the most popular type is chicken. They all supply protein, which our bodies need to build and repair cells, and B vitamins, vital for a healthy nervous system, as well as various minerals (see chart). Unlike red meat, which contains saturated fat, most of the fat in poultry is unsaturated so will not raise blood cholesterol levels. Duck and goose have a higher fat content than chicken and turkey, most of which can be found in the skin and can be removed. For anyone following a low-cholesterol, low-fat diet, skinless chicken or turkey breast with only about 5 per cent fat is an excellent choice. Chicken and turkey livers are a rich source of vitamin A, essential for healthy skin, and of vitamin B_{12}, needed to make the genetic material DNA and RNA in all our cells.

what's in poultry?

roast meat	kcals	protein(g)	fat(g)	vitamins	minerals
CHICKEN				Supplies all the B vitamins, particularly niacin, but only trace amounts of vitamin B_{12}.	Light meat contains slightly more potassium than dark. Dark meat has twice as much iron and zinc as light.
meat and skin	216	23	14		
meat only	148	25	5		
TURKEY				Rich in vitamin B_{12} and a source of the other B vitamins, especially niacin.	Contains potassium and phosphorus and 50 per cent more zinc than chicken.
meat and skin	171	28	7		
meat only	140	29	3		
DUCK				Contains all the B vitamins. Provides more thiamin and riboflavin than chicken.	Supplies three times as much iron as chicken. It is also a good source of potassium and zinc.
meat and skin	339	20	29		
meat only	189	25	10		
GOOSE				Useful source of niacin and contains almost twice as much vitamin B_6 as chicken.	A source of potassium, phosphorus and iron.
meat only	319	29	22		

Nutrients per 100g (3½oz)

If you set a good example, your children will soon learn healthy eating habits that will last a lifetime

children

Children establish eating patterns at an early age and it is up to you to show them that food can be fun *and* healthy. Get off to a good start by encouraging your toddler to explore new tastes – for instance, pear, banana, carrot, fish fingers and bread. Introduce unfamiliar foods one at a time and in small amounts, always ensuring a healthy nutritional balance. Children under five are conservative, so if you meet resistance to certain foods – such as vegetables – try offering others with more appealing colours or textures. Avoid confrontations over food and remember that appetite is often the best guide to your child's nutritional needs. Encourage children to help themselves, but if a child refuses a meal do not offer snacks instead. Under-fives should drink 600ml (1 pint) of whole milk a day for calories and calcium. Do not limit their fat intake (they need the calories) and avoid giving high-fibre foods (which can be difficult to digest).

As children grow, their dietary needs change. To develop strong, healthy bodies, they need more protein and calories. Approximate targets to aim for are: 1,200 Calories a day for a one-year-old, 1,600 for

case study

When she was two, Natasha used to suffer from recurrent throat infections, which necessitated frequent trips to the doctor. Eventually, blood tests revealed that Natasha was deficient in iron. Iron-deficiency anaemia is common among children, accounting for 12 per cent of hospital admissions among Western children and 28 per cent among Asian. The deficiency is mostly mild and dietary shortfalls are usually the problem. Good sources of iron include meat, pulses and dark green vegetables. Natasha was prescribed iron syrup by her doctor, and she was soon back to her old self.

Good basics for a healthy lunchbox that will keep your child going for the best part of the day include cheese, ham and salad sandwiches, fruit, yogurt and a cereal bar.

health tips

1 Avoid confrontations over food.

2 Do not use sweets as a bribe or reward.

3 Include plenty of fruit and vegetables in home-cooked meals.

4 Do not force children to try to eat more than they want.

5 If you use convenience foods, try to alternate them with home-cooked meals.

6 Encourage children to devise and cook their own healthy recipes.

a five-year-old, 2,700 for a 16-year-old boy and 2,100 for a girl of the same age. (Boys need more than girls at all stages, just as men need more than women.)

Teenagers have an increased need for all nutrients, especially during rapid growth periods. Girls tend to have spurts of growth between 10 and 15, and boys between 12 and 19. A good intake of calcium is crucial at such times: three 200ml (7fl oz) glasses of milk and 125ml (4½fl oz) of yogurt would supply nearly all of the recommended 1,000mg daily requirement. Unfortunately, it is quite common for teenagers to start skipping meals at home in favour of fast foods and fizzy drinks. Rather than nagging them, try to discover what they are eating, and redress any imbalances with healthy foods at home. If they become overweight, encourage them to exercise rather than diet excessively.

Adolescent girls, increasingly conscious of their body image, may go on a crash diet or take up a new attitude to food, such as turning vegetarian. Either can lead to iron deficiency at the very time when they need plenty of iron (14.8mg a day). Good non-meat sources of iron include dried apricots, eggs, green vegetables, watercress, wholemeal bread and iron-fortified cereals.

If your child develops a serious problem with food at any stage, seek advice from your GP. Young adulthood normally sees a return to healthier eating habits.

Chocolate and sweets should be enjoyed occasionally, but not eaten as a substitute for more nutritious food

chocolate and sweets

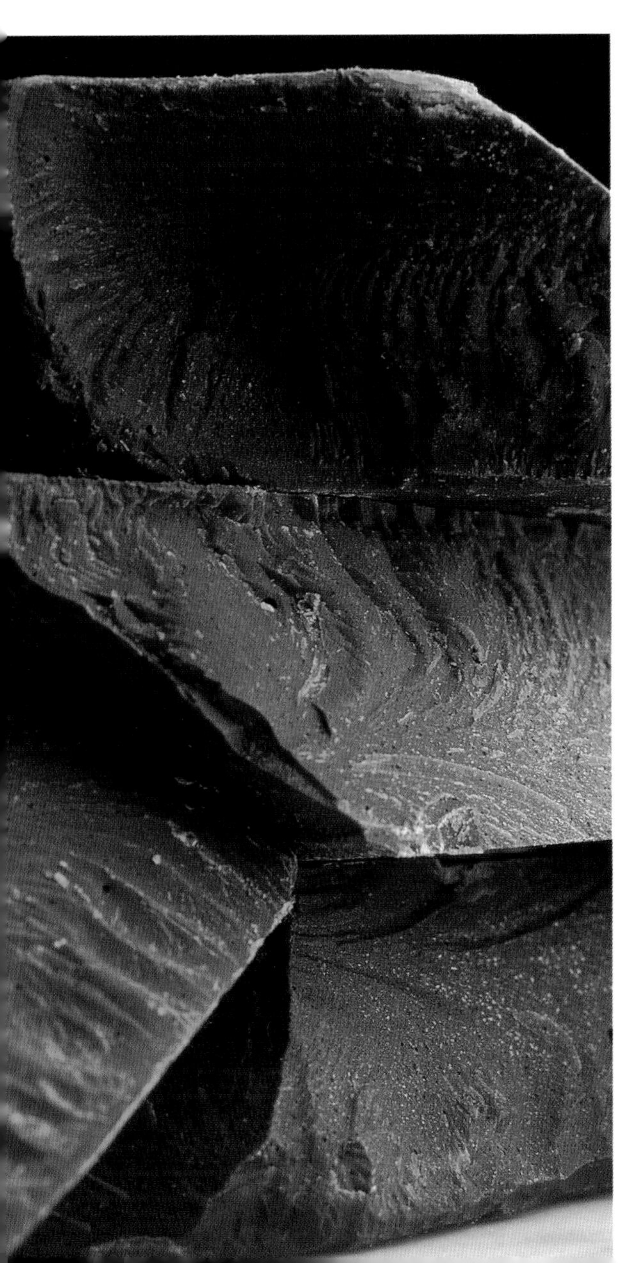

Confectionery comforts us and gives us an instant energy boost, but its nutritional value is usually fairly limited.

Chocolate contains protein, sugar and certain minerals. Plain chocolate has iron and magnesium, and all chocolate contains potassium. Because of its high fat content (30 per cent) chocolate is high in calories: 100g (3½oz) supplies about 500 Calories.

Chocolate also contains stimulants that increase alertness but may cause migraine in some people. Indeed, there is more caffeine in a 125g (4oz) bar of dark chocolate than in a cup of instant coffee. Carob-flavoured confectionery is sold as a healthy alternative to chocolate mainly because it contains no stimulants.

Almost all sweets are high in simple sugars, which deliver a hefty 375 Calories per 100g (3½oz). By satisfying hunger-pangs with empty calories, confectionery can suppress our appetite for a proper meal. ADDITIVES give sweets their bright colours and can cause adverse reactions in susceptible people. And, of course, eating sweets regularly – particularly those that linger in the mouth – causes tooth decay.

health tips

1 **Chocolate tends to be less harmful to teeth than most boiled or chewy sweets.**

2 **Studies show that some chewing gums, sweetened with xylitol rather than sugar, can actually prevent tooth decay.**

Most of us know that high blood cholesterol levels are linked to heart disease. But what exactly is cholesterol?

cholesterol

eat more

1 Wholemeal bread.

2 Wholegrain cereals and oats.

3 Pectin-rich fruit such as grapefruits, dried figs, apricots and prunes.

4 Vegetables such as sweetcorn, mangetout, broad beans and pulses.

5 Garlic and onions.

cut down on

Saturated fats and trans fatty acids, found in:

1 Hard cheese, cream, butter and other full-fat dairy products.

2 Hard margarine and solid cooking fats.

3 Fatty meat and meat products such as hamburgers, salamis, frankfurters and pâtés.

4 Cakes, biscuits, pastries and chocolates.

There are two distinct types of cholesterol that people often confuse: one is found in food, the other is needed for the body's metabolism. Both are fat-like substances.

Dietary cholesterol is contained in foods from animal sources: liver and other offal, egg yolks, and shellfish such as prawns are especially high in cholesterol.

Blood cholesterol is produced by the liver. The fatty, waxy substance forms part of all our body cells and is involved in several functions including making certain hormones, vitamin D and bile acids.

The big threat to a healthy heart is a high blood cholesterol level, which tends to run in families, although diet and obesity are also factors. How much cholesterol you eat is not directly reflected in your blood cholesterol level because the liver reduces its cholesterol output to help compensate when levels from foods become too high.

The best way to lower raised blood cholesterol levels – by as much as 14 per cent, according to a recent study – is to eat less saturated fat. (But anyone with a history of heart disease should also limit their intake of cholesterol-rich foods.) Saturated fats and trans fatty acids (called 'hydrogenated' fats on food labels) should make up only a tenth of your total calories. They are the main fats in meats, full-fat dairy produce, cakes, biscuits, chocolates and any fat that is solid at room temperature.

Eat plenty of wholegrains, oats, pulses (including baked beans), vegetables and fruit, as their soluble fibre helps the body eliminate cholesterol. And include garlic in your diet: it contains compounds that help suppress cholesterol production in the liver.

are you at risk?

If you are concerned about your risk of heart disease, ask your doctor for a blood test to determine your cholesterol levels. Blood cholesterol is measured in millimoles per litre, also expressed as mmol/l, against which susceptibility to heart disease is assessed.

cholesterol level	degree of risk
Below 5.2mmol/l	Low
5.2–6.5mmol/l	Average
6.5–7.8mmol/l	Moderate
Over 7.8mmol/l	High

Your results will be reviewed in the context of other risk factors, such as family medical history and lifestyle, to establish whether any precautionary action is necessary. Regular exercise can reduce heart disease risks, as can two glasses of wine a day (unless you are overweight).

circulation problems

Our circulation system, powered by the heart, enables blood to supply nourishment to all our cells. Although circulation problems can be hereditary, they are also linked to diet. One of the most common is atherosclerosis, where the arteries fur up and harden. This impedes the blood flow and raises blood pressure so the heart has to work harder. There is an increased risk of HEART DISEASE as well as circulation problems such as CRAMP, varicose veins and chilblains. This is much more common among those with raised blood cholesterol. To keep blood cholesterol levels healthy, cut down on saturated fats from animal sources and eat plenty of fibre. Other useful foods include oil-rich fish (discourages blood clotting); potassium-rich foods, such as bananas (for healthy blood pressure); onions, chilli and garlic (facilitate blood flow by increasing blood vessel flexibility); iron-rich foods, such as dark green vegetables (to ensure healthy oxygen levels in the blood). In addition, avoid too much salt or alcohol, which harden the arteries, but exercise regularly to prevent weight gain.

eat more

1 Oil-rich fish (sardines, salmon, mackerel).

2 Wholegrains, fruit and vegetables for fibre.

3 Garlic and onions.

4 Bananas for potassium.

cut down on

1 Alcohol and salt.

2 Fatty meats.

avoid

Smoking.

coeliac disease

This disorder of the intestine tends to run in families and can strike at any age. It is caused by a sensitivity to gluten, a protein found in cereals such as wheat, rye, oats and barley. In susceptible people, gluten damages the villi – tiny frond-like projections that line the small intestine – so that nutrients are not absorbed properly.

Once the disease is diagnosed, the sufferer is prescribed a gluten-free diet. This means he or she must cut out many foods: not only bread, cereals, biscuits and pasta but foods containing breadcrumbs (such as sausages), sauces or soups thickened with wheatflour, prepared foods containing modified starch, and drinks made with barley (beer, stout, malted milk drinks). It means checking every food label.

A dietician will advise on a gluten-free diet, which should include plenty of potatoes, rice, pulses, corn and nuts to replace prohibited foods. To make life easier, many shops now sell a specialised range of gluten-free products, including bread, pasta and biscuits. Cornflour, rice flour or soya flour can be used to thicken sauces.

eat more

1 Potatoes, rice and corn (maize).

2 Lentils, rice, beans, peas and nuts.

avoid

1 Wheat flours – in bread, pasta, cakes and processed foods.

2 Cereals, oats and rye.

3 Sausages and other processed meats.

4 Drinks made with barley, such as beer.

coffee and caffeine

benefit

Can improve mental alertness.

drawbacks

1 Too much brewed or percolated coffee can raise blood cholesterol.

2 May cause insomnia.

3 Excess amounts of coffee can speed up calcium loss.

avoid

Sudden withdrawal: it can cause headaches.

Coffee is rich in caffeine, a stimulant also present in tea, chocolate, colas and some pain-relief tablets. A cup of black coffee has almost no nutritional value, though caffeine increases mental alertness, and stimulates the heart and central nervous system. Medical advice is to drink no more than six cups a day, but those with heart problems should drink less. Coffee can raise blood cholesterol levels if made by a method that extracts the oils, such as cafetière, percolator or espresso. (Instant coffee or coffee that has been filtered through paper are better options.) Coffee is a diuretic, facilitating calcium excretion and increasing risks of OSTEOPOROSIS. It can also act as a laxative, and may cause migraines, insomnia and palpitations.

colds

eat more

1 Fresh fruit, for vitamin C.

2 Zinc-rich foods – oysters, liver (unless you are pregnant), lean meat and pulses.

3 Onion and garlic, which are natural decongestants.

drink more

Fluids, to prevent dehydration.

The best way to boost your immune system and stay free of colds is to eat plenty of fresh fruit and vegetables, and to make time for rest and relaxation. You are more likely to catch a cold when your resistance is low – as a result of poor diet, stress, exhaustion, depression or chronic illness.

Claims by Nobel prizewinner Linus Pauling that large doses of vitamin C can alleviate cold symptoms have not been scientifically proved, but many people find the vitamin helps. At the first sneeze, take 2–3 grams every day for up to seven days (but not if you are pregnant); you can also eat citrus fruits for vitamin C. Zinc-rich foods may be helpful, too: research suggests that zinc helps you shake off a cold faster. Hot chicken soup, the traditional Jewish standby, is easy to digest and provides protein and useful minerals.

Natural remedies include garlic and onion, nasal decongestants that help fight infection; and chillies, ginger and cloves, which also help to clear congested airways. A hot toddy, made with lemons, honey and whisky, will help lull you to sleep.

colitis

The full name for this inflammatory disease of the colon or rectum is ulcerative colitis. It affects one in 20,000 – mainly young adults, and slightly more women than men. When the disease is active, the symptoms include swelling, bleeding and ulceration of the lining of the colon, causing pain and diarrhoea. However, there can be several years between relapses.

The causes are not fully known and there is no cure, but diet can help reduce symptoms. A well-balanced, high-protein diet is vital, particularly after a flare-up or if food intake is reduced to relieve diarrhoea. Plenty of soluble-fibre-rich foods are recommended, but foods high in insoluble fibre (wholegrain cereals, nuts, sweetcorn) should be avoided as they irritate the colon and stimulate bowel contractions. Choose a wide range of foods but avoid any that aggravate the inflammation; studies show that fewer relapses occur on a milk-free diet. Be sure to include sources of vitamins A, C, D, B_{12} and folate, as well as calcium, potassium and zinc. Iron is also important as colitis sufferers often develop ANAEMIA.

eat more

1 **Fruit, beans, lentils and leafy vegetables for soluble fibre.**

2 **Liver (unless pregnant) and sardines for iron.**

3 **Oil-rich fish for vitamin D and omega-3 fatty acids.**

avoid

Foods high in insoluble fibre, such as wholegrain cereals.

constipation

A low-fibre diet, insufficient fluid intake and long periods of inactivity are common causes of constipation, which is characterised by hardened stools and infrequent, often painful bowel movements. Some people wrongly assume they are constipated if they fail to have a daily bowel action. In fact, anything from three times a day to once in three days can be normal and healthy, depending on the individual.

Habitual constipation can cause long-term bowel problems and even lead to colon cancer. To reduce the risks of this, eat plenty of washed but unpeeled fruit, and vegetables and wholegrains, to provide fibre. The body uses this as a bulking agent, to stimulate the muscles of the colon to push digested food through the gut. A diet based on refined foods often leaves you deficient in fibre, so a dense mass of digested food residue accumulates in the colon. The longer the stool stays in the colon, the more dehydrated it becomes, making it difficult to expel. Drinking at least 1.7 litres (3 pints) of water a day will help to counteract this.

eat more

Unpeeled fruit, vegetables, wholegrain cereals, bread and pasta for fibre.

drink more

Water – at least 1.7 litres (3 pints) a day

cut down on

Refined foods, which are low in fibre.

The range and quality of convenience foods are better than ever. Are they as healthy as home-cooked meals?

convenience foods

safety first

1 To avoid any risk of food poisoning from pre-cooked meals, be sure to store them in a refrigerator or freezer as soon as possible after buying. Also, make sure the food is thoroughly reheated before serving.

2 Be wary of hot take-away meals that are prepared well ahead and kept warm for long periods: they may contain food-poisoning bacteria.

Curries, lasagne, cauliflower cheese, salmon en croûte...We are now spoilt for choice with ready-made packaged meals – and we seem to be increasingly happy to rely on them. They are time-saving and convenient, particularly for people living alone, busy professionals and families who like to eat different things at different times. We expect to pay a price for convenience, but do we pay a price nutritionally?

There is often little to choose between pre-prepared and home-cooked meals in terms of their nutrient value. Most convenience foods (whether instant-pudding mix or ready-to-eat meals) give full details of their ingredients on the labels. Watch out for sugar, salt and fat levels, and if concerned about any of these, opt for one of the many 'healthy', calorie-counted varieties now available.

Remember that any pre-cooked meals – whether made the night before at home or bought in the supermarket – will have lost some nutrients in the initial cooking and may lose more when reheated. So it makes sense to supplement your meal with extra freshly cooked vegetables, salad or fruit.

Occasional take-away, ready-to-eat foods – anything from a burger and chips to a tuna-and-salad sandwich – can form part of a healthy diet. Use your knowledge of nutrition to guide you. In a burger bar, for example, you can limit your intake of calories and fat by choosing a burger without cheese, salad without mayonnaise, a small portion of french fries, and milk, rather than a milk shake. Unlike packaged-food manufacturers, fast-food sellers do not have to list the ingredients used, but some will give you an information sheet if asked.

The important thing, as always, is to ensure you are balancing your diet and eating a good variety of foods. If you rely heavily on convenience or fast foods your diet is likely to be high in sugar, salt and fat, low in fibre and short on vitamin C, iron, folate and riboflavin. But, with a little forethought, it is easy to strike a healthy balance between pre-prepared and home-cooked meals. A herb omelette with salad and a wholemeal roll, for example, takes only minutes to prepare and would be a healthy lunch to balance with a heat-and-eat chicken curry and rice at supper.

courgettes and marrows

Unlike marrows, their larger relatives, courgettes have tender, edible skins, so you can benefit from the nutrients they contain. A lightly boiled 100g (3½oz) portion of courgettes is a good choice for weight watchers as it provides only 19 Calories – as opposed to 63 Calories if fried in oil. Yet it contains a quarter of the vitamin C and almost one-sixth of the folate an adult needs each day, as well as beta carotene, which the body converts to vitamin A, and potassium, which helps to regulate blood pressure. The same portion of courgettes served raw (in a salad, for example) would supply twice as much vitamin C and about a quarter of the daily folate requirement. There is very little nutritional difference between green and yellow courgettes.

Marrow is 95.6 per cent water. It contains exactly the same nutrients as courgettes, but in smaller quantities. Its main virtue is its low calorie count: a 100g (3½oz) portion of lightly boiled, pale green marrow flesh provides a mere 9 Calories. More nutrients are gained if you eat the skin, but it is generally much too tough.

benefits

1 **Low in calories.**

2 **Contain vitamin C, folate, beta carotene and potassium.**

cramp

eat more

1 Calcium-rich foods such as dairy products and sardines eaten with their bones.

2 Wholegrain cereals, nuts and seeds, for magnesium.

3 Avocados, nuts and seeds for vitamin E; eggs and fish for vitamin B_{12}; leafy green vegetables for iron.

cut down on

Saturated fats.

A sudden painful spasm in a muscle is called cramp. It occurs when local circulation fails, starving the muscle of oxygen and causing a build-up of lactic acid, a waste product. Massage and gentle stretching are the best treatment, but nutrition can play an effective role in prevention.

When cramp occurs after vigorous exercise, particularly in hot or humid weather, it is because excessive sweating causes dehydration and loss of sodium. An isotonic drink will help to replace lost fluids and salts. However, drinking plenty of water (about 1 litre or 1¾ pints per hour of activity) before, during and after exercise will prevent dehydration in the first place.

Calcium and magnesium are needed for muscle contraction, so include sources of both in your diet. Foods high in vitamins E and B_{12} may help protect against night cramps, and iron-rich foods will ward off ANAEMIA, another cause of cramp. Calf pains when walking briskly can be due to narrowed arteries: limit intake of saturated fats to reduce the risk. Severe or recurring cramp may indicate heart disease.

cranberries

benefits

1 Help to fight bladder, kidney and urinary-tract infections.

2 Anti-viral properties that help the body to resist disease.

3 Source of vitamin C.

drawback

Commercially produced cranberry juice often has a high sugar content.

These red berries are native to North America, where as well as being valued for their vitamin C and anti-viral properties they have long been used as a traditional remedy for bladder, kidney and urinary-tract infections, including CYSTITIS. The bacterium that commonly causes these sorts of infections is *E. coli*, which thrives by attaching itself to the cells lining the walls of the bladder and urinary tract. Recent research in the USA suggests that an unidentified substance found in cranberries prevents the bacteria from taking hold and multiplying. Many urologists now recommend 450ml (16fl oz) of cranberry juice a day to prevent and control mild urinary-tract infections. Like many fruit drinks, cranberry juice often contains a lot of sugar.

Snacks can satisfy hunger pangs and boost flagging energy levels, but some are healthier than others

crisps and snacks

Savoury snacks are not renowned for their nutrient provision as many have a high salt and fat content (much of it saturated). In moderation, they do you no harm, especially if you balance them with the day's nutrient requirements. After a low-fat, wholemeal-bread sandwich and an orange for lunch, for example, you need not worry about eating a bag of crisps (which contain some potassium and vitamin C). But if you regularly dine on crisps and chocolate your diet will be unbalanced, and this could ultimately undermine your health.

Examine the labels of all manufactured savoury snacks for calories. A 50g (2oz) packet of nuts may provide 300 Calories – the equivalent of a small meal. Try to match your calorie intake with your body's everyday energy demands, and avoid high-calorie snacks if your lifestyle is sedentary. Labels also give the fat and salt content. For example, an average bag of tortilla chips usually contains about 11g of fat, and a 30g packet of crisps about 10g. Both of them are high in salt, which is often expressed as sodium on the labels (1g of sodium equals 2.5g of salt).

health tips

Healthy alternatives to crisps as between-meal snacks include:

1 Fresh fruit.

2 Raw vegetables, eaten with or without low-calorie dips.

3 Low-fat yogurt, with or without honey or wheatgerm.

4 Dried fruit.

5 Unsalted nuts.

6 Oatcakes, ricecakes or crispbreads with cottage cheese.

When you cannot absorb nutrients and certain foods upset you, it is vital to guard against malnourishment

crohn's disease

food note

A supervised exclusion diet can help identify problem foods. With your doctor's guidance, you can try eliminating foods one by one from your diet, to see if this brings about any improvement.

Crohn's disease, a chronic inflammatory bowel condition that can affect any part of the gastrointestinal tract, is most likely to develop between the ages of 15 and 35. Symptoms, which can fluctuate in severity, include fever, abdominal pain and diarrhoea. The causes of Crohn's disease are not fully understood, and there is as yet no cure, but medical treatment usually involves steroids. Surgery may be required to remove affected areas of the intestine.

Weight loss is a common problem with this condition: lack of appetite, a feeling of nausea and crampy pain on eating can make it difficult to face meals. In addition, absorption of nutrients is often impaired by the scarred, thickened wall of the intestine, and the inflammation can trigger nutrient loss. A nutritious diet is essential to avoid vitamin and mineral deficiencies. Foods rich in omega-3 fatty acids (such as oil-rich fish) are said by some nutritionists to be helpful. Exclude only those foods that make symptoms worse. Food intolerance (see ALLERGIES) is now thought to be a factor in Crohn's disease: grains, yeast, dairy products, nuts, shellfish, raw fruit and pickles are the foods most often cited.

Joe is 22 and suffers from Crohn's disease. He has had recurrent episodes of diarrhoea, abdominal pain, nausea, fatigue and fever. Six months ago, Joe consulted his doctor for dietary advice. He was told that aspirin and antibiotics can be triggers, and that milk products, preservatives and cereals can also spark attacks. As Crohn's disease can cause anaemia, the doctor recommended that Joe include plenty of iron-rich foods in his diet. Since then Joe has identified dairy produce as one cause of his flare-ups, and has noticed some improvement since reducing his intake of milky drinks.

cystic fibrosis

This hereditary, life-threatening disease is caused by a defect in the gene controlling the passage of salt and water across the body's cell membranes. The lungs and pancreas are especially affected, becoming clogged with thick, sticky mucus.

Cystic fibrosis makes enormous energy demands on the body. A nutritious high-protein, high-calorie diet is essential, both to help ward off chest infections and to compensate for the fact that food is not properly digested and absorbed because of a lack of pancreatic enzymes (protein and fat tend to be lost in the stools).

People with cystic fibrosis need about twice the normal daily requirement of protein and up to twice the calories, though they often have poor appetites. They should therefore eat as much protein, fat and carbohydrate as they can, and supplement meals with calorie-rich snacks. Fatty foods and whole milk are recommended.

eat more

1 High-protein foods (meat, poultry and fish).

2 Fats, including full-fat dairy products, fatty fish and oils.

3 Starchy foods (bread, potatoes, pasta) and sugary foods (honey, jam, cakes and sweets).

avoid

Low-calorie and reduced-fat foods.

cystitis

Although men are occasional victims, it is mainly women who suffer from cystitis. This painful bladder infection makes you keep wanting to urinate, but whenever you try you can pass only a tiny amount, which causes a burning sensation. Sufferers should drink at least 2 litres (3½ pints) of water or other non-alcoholic fluids a day. This dilutes the acidity of the urine, so urinating becomes less painful.

Studies show that cranberries can help to prevent cystitis. They contain a substance that discourages the offending bacterium *E. coli* from sticking to the walls of the urinary tract. Tests have shown that drinking a glass of cranberry juice a day helps to prevent the infection starting, even among regular cystitis sufferers. There is also some evidence that a daily portion of cranberries, or about 450ml (15fl oz) of juice, can help to treat cystitis. If symptoms persist, you should seek medical advice.

Certain foods have been known to aggravate cystitis symptoms in some people, particularly very spicy or chilli-hot foods, tea, coffee and fizzy drinks.

drink more

1 Water – at least 2 litres (3½ pints a day).

2 Cranberry juice.

avoid

1 Food containing chilli or spices.

2 Tea, coffee and fizzy drinks.

dates

benefits

1 Fresh and dried dates are high in fibre so help prevent constipation.

2 Dried dates are rich in potassium, which helps maintain the body's fluid balance and regulate blood pressure, heartbeat, and nerve and muscle function.

drawback

Dried dates are high in sugar, increasing the risk of tooth decay.

Fresh dates are a far cry from the sticky dried dates we associate with Christmas. The fresh fruits are a useful source of vitamin C – vital for the immune system – and 100g (3½oz) provides nearly a third of the adult daily requirement. Drying dates concentrates their nutrients, except for the vitamin C, which is destroyed in the process. Vitamin C aside, drying turns them into a rich source of potassium, essential for maintaining the body's fluid balance and blood pressure, and for regulating the heartbeat and nerve and muscle function. But drying also concentrates their sugar content, increasing the risk of tooth decay, and raises their calorie value: whereas 100g (3½oz) of fresh dates contains 107 Calories, the same weight of dried dates contains 227 Calories.

Both dried and fresh dates contain useful amounts of soluble fibre, which can help to relieve constipation and reduce blood cholesterol levels. Dates have been found to contain tyramine, a substance that also occurs in some cheeses, which can cause migraine in susceptible people.

diabetes

eat more

High-fibre foods (beans, peas, lentils, vegetables, fruit, oats) and complex carbohydrate foods to slow the rate at which sugar is released into the bloodstream.

cut down on

1 Salt and salty foods.

2 Fried foods and fatty foods.

3 High-sugar foods, which raise blood sugar levels too quickly.

Diabetes is a disease characterised by the body's inability to regulate blood sugar levels. Sugar, which is the body's main source of energy, is distributed via the bloodstream as glucose. To keep the body working in peak condition, the levels of glucose must be carefully controlled, and this is the job of the pancreas. When high blood sugar levels are detected, the pancreas secretes insulin to remove some of the glucose and store it in the liver and muscles. If this process is impaired in some way, the excess glucose is excreted – so one symptom of diabetes is high sugar levels in the urine. Others include excessive thirst, needing to go to the loo frequently, weight loss, exhaustion, low resistance to other illnesses, and impaired vision.

There are two types of diabetes. Type 1, insulin-dependent diabetes mellitus or IDDM, is caused by damage to the insulin-producing cells in the pancreas. Type 2, non-insulin-dependent diabetes mellitus or NIDDM, is much more common in older people and stems from increasing failure of the body to recognise insulin – initially causing the pancreas to produce more. Being overweight can bring about the onset of Type 2, as can a lack of exercise, and it can often be treated simply by a change of diet and lifestyle. Type 1 must be treated with regular insulin injections but although the cause is not diet related, a special diet can still help regulate blood sugar levels.

General advice for sufferers of both types includes eating plenty of foods high in complex carbohydrate and fibre, to slow down sugar release into the blood, plus avoiding foods high in fats and sugar. Eating frequently and regularly is important. Be sure to check what you drink, too, as some manufactured drinks are high in sugar. Water and sugar-free drinks are best.

Diabetes predisposes sufferers to other conditions such as heart disease, high blood pressure, kidney failure and deteriorating eyesight. Limiting salt intake will help guard against raised blood pressure, and keeping a strict eye on fat consumption will help reduce the likelihood of coronary heart disease. Your doctor or dietician will help you tailor a diet to suit your needs.

diarrhoea

An attack of diarrhoea is usually the body's way of hurrying food along the intestine to rid itself of an irritant, such as a bacterial or viral infection. So it makes sense not to eat for 24 hours to give your system time to recover, but increase the amount you drink to replace lost fluids and salts. Very dilute fruit drinks are adequate for mild attacks: in more severe cases, make up a rehydration solution of 8 teaspoons of sugar and 1 teaspoon of salt to 1 litre (1¾ pt) of boiled water – or buy ready-mixed sachets from the chemist. Once you start to feel better, try a few bland foods: bananas, white rice, stewed apples and white toast (the 'BRAT' diet). Bananas are easily digested and high in potassium, which is lost when you are dehydrated; white rice and toast provide carbohydrates without fibre – the last thing you need – and stewed apple contains pectin, which helps liquids gel. Gradually reintroduce a normal diet 48 hours later. Avoid tea, coffee and alcohol for a few days, as these diuretics may undo the effort you have put into rehydrating your body.

drink more

Very dilute fruit drinks or rehydration solutions.

avoid

All food for 24 hours, and tea, coffee and alcohol for a few days.

safety first

Diarrhoea in babies, small children and the elderly can quickly lead to dehydration. Always seek medical advice.

Forget about short, sharp, self-denial routines and adopt healthy eating and exercise patterns to last a lifetime

diets and slimming

eat more

1 **Carbohydrates such as potatoes, bread, rice, pasta and cereals.**

2 **Fresh fruit and vegetables.**

3 **Low-fat versions of foods such as cheese, yogurt, milk and dairy spreads.**

cut down on

1 **Fatty foods such as sausages, bacon, mince, cakes, pies, biscuits, crisps and nuts.**

2 **Alcohol, which is high in calories.**

Following a diet to lose weight implies that sooner or later you can stop the diet and go back to what you used to eat. But the only way to lose weight and keep it off is to change your eating habits permanently.

Although there is no need to conform to the 'ideal' shape promoted by fashion magazines, there is ample evidence that being overweight is actually unhealthy. Obesity – defined by the medical profession as being 30 per cent heavier than is typical for your height, age, sex, frame and height – can increase the risk of high blood pressure, diabetes, gout, angina, gallstones, arthritis, and joint damage from carrying all that extra weight on your frame.

To lose weight, your body basically needs to expend more energy (measured in calories) than it takes in as food. This means eating fewer calories and taking more exercise. The foods highest in calories are FATS, with 9 Calories per gram; carbohydrates, by contrast, have fewer than half as many – 4 Calories per gram. So by restricting fats and increasing the amount of carbohydrates you eat, you can work out a diet to help you to lose weight with the minimum hardship. (In the past, calorie-counting was considered the best way to keep track of what you had eaten every day; now it is considered to be old-fashioned, and it is also unnecessary if you stick to the principles explained here.) Carbohydrates such as potatoes, pasta, rice and bread are all filling foods that can be eaten in reasonable quantities, so you are unlikely to go hungry. You can eat unlimited amounts of vegetables and fresh fruit as long as you refrain from adding lashings of cream, butter, mayonnaise or fatty sauces.

Protein is an essential part of all diets. Red meat often comes with fat attached, but you can easily trim it off. Chicken is also far less fatty with its skin removed. Cook them in ways that will not add fat: instead of frying try grilling and baking. Avoid meats with hidden fat content, such as sausages and minced beef. Choose white fish occasionally instead of fattier oil-rich fish. And go for low-fat cheeses, natural yogurts and skimmed milk.

Once you have reached your target weight, you can gradually adjust your intake so that your weight remains stable.

A well-balanced diet leads to healthy digestion – but if problems do occur, what you eat can ease the symptoms

digestion

Our digestive system is designed to break down food in stages, with different nutrients extracted at every step. As long as we eat a balanced and healthy diet with plenty of fresh fruit and vegetables, the digestive system should function smoothly.

Digestion really begins with chewing, which breaks down food into pieces small enough for stomach enzymes to get to work on easily. Even as we chew, saliva immediately starts to break down any starch present before food reaches the stomach. Once in the stomach, acids, enzymes and muscle action begin to break down proteins and transform food into a semi-liquid sludge, which eventually moves along into the small intestine. Here the pancreas releases digestive juices that break down protein still further, while bile from the gall bladder emulsifies the fats present. Most of the nutrients that our bodies require are absorbed into the bloodstream via the lining of the small intestine, which is covered in millions of tiny fronds that vastly increase its surface area to allow maximum nutrient uptake. Anything that reaches the large intestine will not be digested further: fibre, for example, bulks

eat more

Fresh fruit and vegetables.

drink more

Water – about 1.7 litres (3 pints) a day will help keep digested food residue moving through the system.

cut down on

1 Refined carbohydrates.

2 Fatty foods (especially fried ones), which can overload the digestive process.

3 Alcohol, which can cause inflammation of the stomach wall.

case study

Sarah, a secretary aged 35, was a 20-a-day smoker who enjoyed a glass of wine in the evening. In the past year she had put on a stone in weight. But only when she noticed symptoms of heart-burn, nausea, stomach pains and an acid taste in her mouth did she visit her GP. Her doctor diagnosed acid reflux from her stomach and oesophagus, and advised her to change her diet, smoke and drink less and lose weight. By cutting down on fatty foods, citrus fruits, spices, alcohol and coffee, and eating frequent small meals, Sarah lost half a stone in three months and her symptoms have all but gone.

out waste products together with water, making them easier to push through the gut and, ultimately, out of the body.

Hiccups tend to occur only when a diet is heavy in over-refined, processed foods, often coupled with too much tea, coffee, sweetened drinks or alcohol.

Indigestion, wind and constipation can all be warning signs that the digestive system is overloaded – and these complaints can usually all be helped enormously by improvements to your diet. Indigestion is caused by too much acid in the stomach,

A 48-hour diet of bland foods – nothing but bananas, apples, boiled white rice and dry white toast – and plenty of water will help anyone with gastroenteritis.

what to eat

Digestive problems can often be eased by a change of diet. If the disorder is severe or does not respond to the new diet after a few days, consult your doctor.

foods to forgo	foods to eat
COELIAC DISEASE	
Wheat or cereals with gluten, flour products, tinned foods with flour as a thickener, and beer.	Fresh fruit and vegetables, pulses, nuts, poultry, cheese, rice and potatoes.
COLITIS (INCLUDING CROHN'S DISEASE)	
Wheat bran, nuts, seeds, sweetcorn and all foods known to contain substances to which you are susceptible.	Porridge, apples, parsley, dried fruit, oil-rich fish, liver, lentils, watercress. Extra zinc, calcium, magnesium, B vitamins and vitamins C and K may also be needed.
DIVERTICULAR DISEASE	
Refined carbohydrates: replace them with wholegrain types.	Cooked leafy vegetables, wholemeal bread, brown rice, wholegrain cereals, porridge and apples.
GASTROENTERITIS	
For the first 48 hours, avoid all foods except those listed opposite.	Bananas, apples, boiled white rice and dry white toast. Plenty of water to replace lost fluids.
INDIGESTION	
All acid foods (particularly those made with vinegar), raw onions, chillies, fatty or fried foods, coffee and alcohol.	Fibre-rich wholemeal bread, brown rice and vegetables.
IRRITABLE BOWEL SYNDROME	
Wheat bran, pulses and any specific foods to which you have an allergy or intolerance.	Fruit and vegetables for their soluble fibre, and live natural yogurt for its friendly bacteria.
WIND	
Try to cut down on peas, beans and lentils, as well as Brussels sprouts and cabbage.	Live yogurt, peppermint and fennel teas. Thyme, sage, caraway and fennel seeds all help digestion.

leading to heartburn. The acids actually rise up into the oesophagus (the tube that connects stomach and mouth). Alcohol, fatty foods, acidic pickles and coffee can all make things worse. Wind is the natural result of intestinal bacteria breaking down undigested carbohydrates and proteins, but excessive amounts may be a symptom of an underlying illness such as an ULCER or Crohn's disease. To avoid CONSTIPATION make sure you drink plenty of water – at least 1.7 litres (3 pints) a day – as well as plenty of fruit and vegetables, wholegrain cereals and wholemeal bread. A sedentary lifestyle doesn't help either, so if your job keeps you deskbound, make sure you take some form of exercise regularly.

More serious problems associated with the digestive system – COELIAC DISEASE, COLITIS, CROHN'S DISEASE, diverticular disease and IRRITABLE BOWEL SYNDROME – can significantly reduce the absorption of nutrients from the gut. These conditions obviously need medical treatment, but avoiding certain foods and eating more of others helps control them, too (see chart).

eczema

One in 10 people in Britain has eczema, a skin condition characterised by inflamed, dry and flaking skin and severe itching. There are two main types. Contact eczema (or contact dermatitis) occurs when skin is sensitive to irritants such as wool, make-up, or detergents. Atopic eczema, the more prevalent type, affects people with a family history of allergy such as ASTHMA or hay fever, and is most common in childhood.

Eczema can be triggered or aggravated by a variety of allergens, and often several are involved. Food may be a trigger for one in three children with eczema. The chief culprits are cow's milk and eggs, followed by soya, wheat, fish and shellfish, and nuts.

Pinpointing trigger foods can be difficult, and no test is 100 per cent reliable. One laborious but effective way is to exclude suspect foods from your diet for two weeks, and if the condition improves, to reintroduce the foods one by one. If symptoms return, you have probably identified a food with an allergen that is causing the eczema. Always consult a GP or dietician before eliminating foods from your diet.

avoid

Any foods that trigger or aggravate symptoms. Possible culprits include:

1 **Cow's milk and eggs.**

2 **Wheat and soya products.**

3 **Fish and shellfish.**

4 **Nuts.**

5 **Tomatoes.**

6 **Yeast.**

7 **Certain additives.**

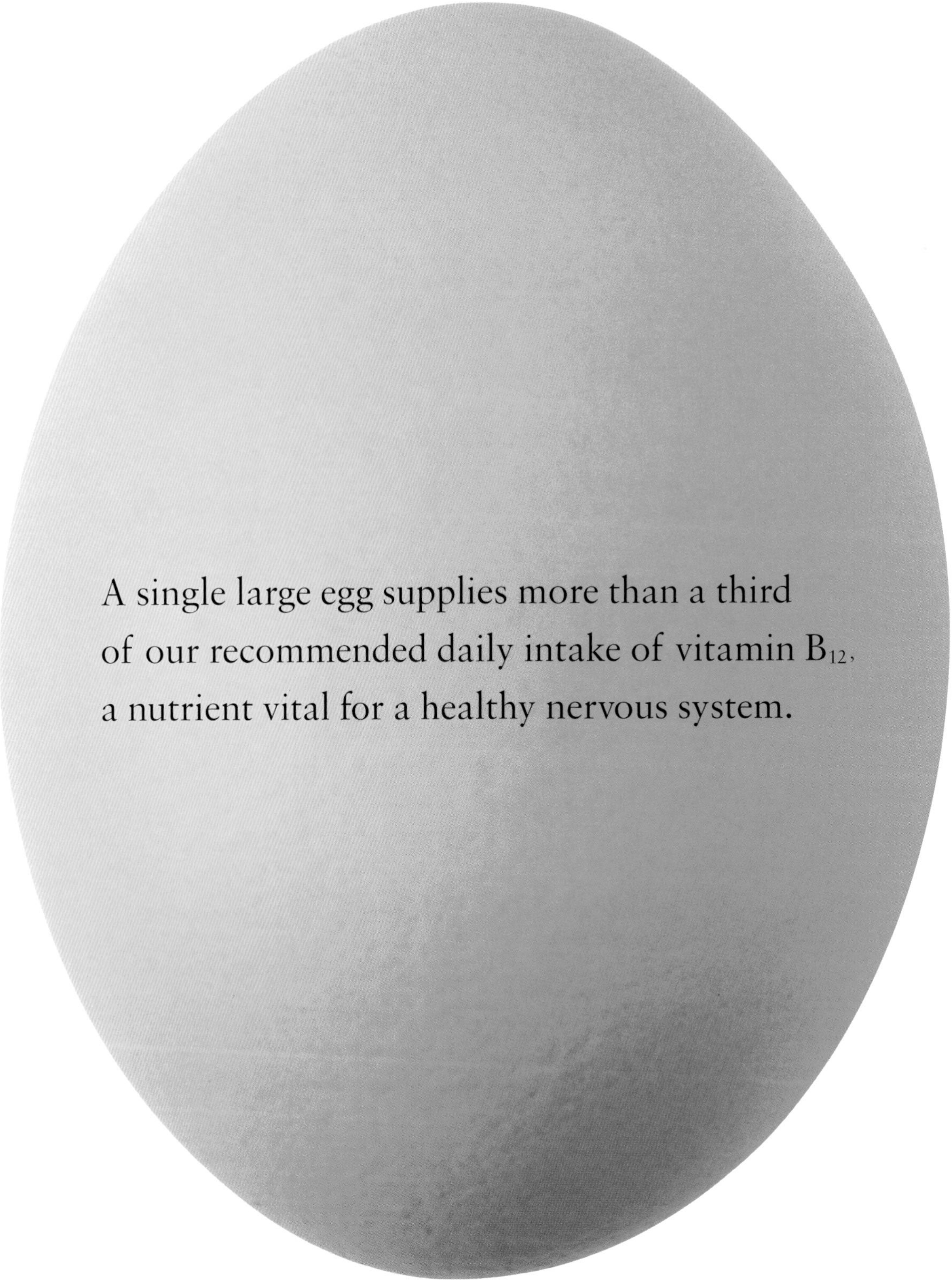

A single large egg supplies more than a third of our recommended daily intake of vitamin B_{12}, a nutrient vital for a healthy nervous system.

Designed to nourish, an egg provides protein, vitamins and minerals, and is still an inexpensive family favourite

eggs

Eggs are the ultimate natural convenience food. They are a good, cheap source of protein, and the yolks are high in minerals – among them zinc, calcium and iron. They also contain vitamins A, D and the B group – particularly vitamin B_{12}, which is vital for a healthy nervous system: a single large egg supplies more than a third of our recommended daily intake.

Eggs are high in CHOLESTEROL: one large egg contains 200mg. However, this does not necessarily mean that eggs are bad for your heart. It is usually blood cholesterol, rather than dietary cholesterol, that is the key factor in the development of heart disease. Blood cholesterol rises when we eat too much saturated fat, and a single large egg contains less than 2g of this. Only people with high blood cholesterol levels need to pay close attention to their dietary cholesterol intake. In 1999 an American study confirmed that eating an egg a day is unlikely to affect blood cholesterol levels unless you have a family history of raised levels. Furthermore, the lecithin in egg yolk contains choline, which helps the body to remove cholesterol from the bloodstream. Opinions, however, remain divided as to how many eggs it is safe to eat. The British Heart Foundation advises no more than four a week, while the World Health Organisation claims that as many as ten will do you no harm.

All eggs sold in supermarkets are carefully checked and date stamped. The lion quality mark on an egg box guarantees the eggs have been produced to even higher standards than required by law.

In rare instances eggs harbour salmonella bacteria, which can cause FOOD POISONING. Those most at risk are children, pregnant women, and ill or elderly people. If you take a few precautions, the chances of infection are slim. To be safe, government advice is never to eat raw eggs or foods made from them, such as mayonnaise or mousses. (Most manufactured products are made from eggs that have been pasteurised to kill bacteria.) Thorough cooking of eggs, until both the white and yolk are solid, will destroy bacteria, and so remove any possible risk of infection from eating runny eggs. Always store eggs in the refrigerator, pointed end down.

benefits

1 Convenient source of protein.

2 Good source of vitamin B_{12}, particularly for vegetarians.

3 Contain vitamins and minerals.

drawbacks

1 High cholesterol content, which could affect those with high blood cholesterol.

2 May cause salmonella poisoning if not thoroughly cooked.

3 In rare instances, may trigger asthma, eczema or allergic reactions in susceptible people.

With the right foods, regular exercise and plenty of rest, you can live life to the full and ward off illness

energy and vitality

eat more

1 Starchy foods – such as wholemeal bread, pasta, potatoes and brown rice – for a steady stream of energy.

2 Snacks such as bananas, dried apricots and raisins for a healthy energy boost.

cut down on

Caffeine and alcohol: in excess, either can interfere with a vital requirement for energy production – your sleep.

health tip

Fatigue may be an early-warning sign of an unsatisfactory diet. If in doubt, consult your doctor.

The best way to achieve that sense of wellbeing that lets you breeze through every challenge – and still have energy to spare – is to combine high-energy, low-fat foods with regular exercise and rest.

Food is the fuel that our bodies convert into energy. We need energy for muscle movement, for the activity of essential organs, for growth and repair – and for living. Energy is measured in calories. Men generally require more than women. Recommended daily intakes are 2,500 and 2,000 Calories respectively. However, individual needs vary significantly depending on age, on how active we are, and on our basal metabolic rate or BMR. Our BMR determines how efficiently we burn energy for our body's basic functions – functions that account for almost 90 per cent of our total energy needs.

The main sources of energy in our diet are carbohydrates, fats and proteins. While 1g of protein or carbohydrate provides 4 Calories, fat supplies 9 Calories per gram. So a high-fat diet makes it all too easy to consume more energy than we need. Government advice is that we should derive 50 per cent of our total energy from carbohydrates. Starchy carbohydrates, such as potatoes, cereals and bread, are an especially good source of sustained physical energy. Athletes choose starchy foods to build up energy reserves. However, these foods can also have a sedative effect on mental energy. A light meal such as grilled fish and salad will leave you feeling alert, whereas a meal based on starchy foods can make you sleepy. (See also MOOD AND DIET.)

Most adults consume just under 2,000 Calories. If you eat more food than your body uses for energy – which many of us do – the surplus calories are stored as fat, and you may become overweight. Initially this may simply sap your vitality, but eventually it may lead to obesity and an increased risk of HEART DISEASE and other serious health problems. To avoid this, try to combine a balanced, low-fat diet with regular aerobic exercise, such as brisk walking. This speeds up breathing and heart rates, and helps to burn off body fat. It also stimulates the release of endorphins, chemicals in the brain that make you feel calmer and happier.

Most of us eat too much 'unhealthy' saturated fat and not enough 'healthy' unsaturated fat

fats

Without fats we would not be able to live. They provide essential fatty acids, which are vital to the body's metabolism; they allow us to harness the fat-soluble vitamins A, D, E and K; and they provide us with a concentrated source of energy – 1g of fat contains 9 Calories, more than twice that provided by protein or carbohydrate. Eaten in excess, however, certain fats can actually damage our health, making us more vulnerable to heart disease and obesity.

Different types of fat

The two main types of fat are saturated and unsaturated. Most foods contain at least some fat, but the proportions of saturated and unsaturated can vary widely. Saturated fats are found mainly in animal products – such as meat, cheese, cream and butter – but are also present in biscuits, cakes and crisps. Most of us in the UK eat more saturated fat than we should, which can lead to high blood CHOLESTEROL levels and an increased risk of obesity and of HEART DISEASE. So we should cut down on saturated fat (especially since the body can make its own when it is needed).

Unsaturated fats come in two forms: monounsaturates, found in nuts, avocados and olive oil, for example; and polyunsaturates, found in foods such as oil-rich fish and vegetable oils. Polyunsaturates are important in the diet because they include

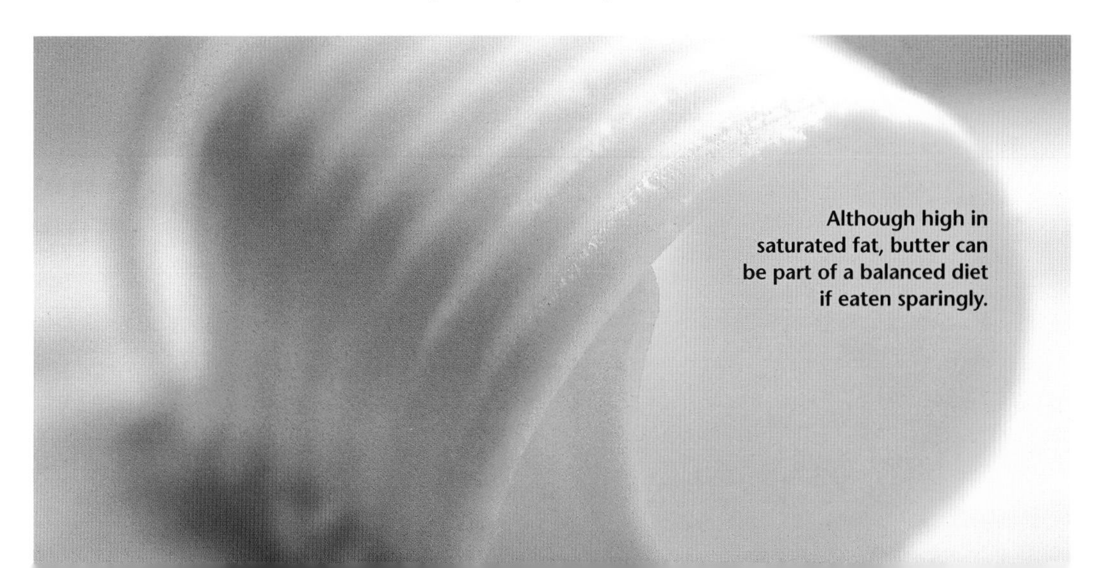

Although high in saturated fat, butter can be part of a balanced diet if eaten sparingly.

benefits

1 Rich source of calories and energy.

2 Enable the body to make use of fat-soluble vitamins A, D, E and K.

drawbacks

1 High intakes of saturated fats can raise blood cholesterol levels and increase the risk of heart disease.

2 Calorie-rich, high-fat diets may lead to obesity.

essential fatty acids that the body cannot manufacture itself. There are two main types of these: omega-6s, found in corn and sunflower oil, and omega-3s, found in oil-rich fish such as sardines or mackerel. They control many functions, including blood flow and inflammation. Omega-3s are necessary for brain development in the foetus, and can prevent blood clots. Too much omega-6 polyunsaturated fat, however, may predispose people to asthma.

When vegetable oils are processed, or 'hydrogenated', to convert them into a semi-solid form, like margarines, some of the unsaturated fats are turned into trans fats or hydrogenated vegetable fats. Although these fats are unsaturated, they behave more like saturated fats in the body, so we need to limit how much we eat. Trans fats can also occur naturally in some foods.

How much fat is too much?

Ideally, fat should provide us with no more than one third of the total calories in our diet – but most people in the UK eat more than this. In other words, if a man consumes the recommended 2,500 Calories a

what sort of fat?

types of fat	found in	what they do
SATURATED FATS	Butter, lard, hard cheeses, fatty meats and meat products, coconut oil and palm oil.	Provide energy. Make vitamins A, D, E and K available to the body. Too much saturated fat can lead to heart disease.
UNSATURATED FATS MONOUNSATURATES	Vegetable oils such as olive oil and rape seed oil. Foods such as avocados, nuts and seeds.	Provide energy. May help to reduce levels of harmful blood cholesterol.
POLYUNSATURATES omega-6 fatty acids	Olive oil, sunflower oil and corn oil; almonds and walnuts.	Provide energy. May reduce levels of artery-clogging blood cholesterol. Omega-3s reduce blood clotting and inflammation. Omega-6s are needed as part of the make-up of all cells. Polyunsaturates must be derived from food sources: the body cannot make its own.
omega-3 fatty acids	Oil-rich fish such as sardines, salmon, herring, mackerel; soya bean and rapeseed oil; walnuts.	
TRANS FATTY ACIDS	Cakes, biscuits, pies and crisps; beef, mutton and dairy products; hydrogenated oils and margarines.	Provide energy. Act like saturated fats in the body.

Use the information on food labels to monitor your daily fat intake. Ideally, no more than 10 per cent of your total daily calories should be derived from saturated fats; 20 per cent should come from unsaturated sources.

day, only 830 of them should be from fat. That's the equivalent of about 90g of fat. Women, whose calorie requirement is slightly lower, should try not to exceed 75g. If you want to keep an eye on your fat intake, read the food labels. The nutrition information panel details the total amount of fat in food, and often the amounts of saturates, monounsaturates and polyunsaturates, too. Nutritionists recommend that saturated fats should make up only about a third of total daily fat intake. The rest should be derived from unsaturated fats.

How to cut down on saturated fat

As a general rule, most of us eat far more saturated fat than is healthy: we need to replace at least some of this 'unhealthy' fat with the healthier, unsaturated types. Use olive oil for cooking rather than hard fats, for example. Try substituting fat-free, or virtually fat-free, milk for full-fat varieties (but not in infants' diets). Opt for a low-fat spread that is high in polyunsaturates, rather than butter. Try to eat oil-rich fish in preference to red meat. And when you do eat meat, trim off any excess fat.

food note

Fats can make food more palatable, giving it a smooth, creamy texture.

fever

A fever or raised temperature is usually a sign that the body is fighting off an infection. Although this is a useful reaction to deal with an invading virus, a fever can become serious, so it is a good idea to take steps to reduce it (with paracetamol, for example), especially in children, who can suffer convulsions. A high temperature will cause sweating and ultimately dehydration. Plenty of cool, clear fluids are recommended, in frequent, small sips if nausea is a symptom. Fever is often accompanied by reduced appetite and can leave the body short on vital nutrients. Forget the old adage 'Feed a cold, starve a fever': provided they are not suffering from diarrhoea or vomiting, recovering patients should be coaxed into eating light, nourishing meals.

Normal body temperature is around 37°C (98.6°F): always consult a doctor whenever a baby has a temperature above 38.5°C (101.3°F), or a child or adult registers 39.4°C (102.9°F). Seek medical help at once if a fever persists for more than three days or is combined with other distressing symptoms such as severe pain.

drink more

Water to replace fluids lost in sweating. Aim for at least 1.7 litres (3 pints) a day to avoid dehydration.

An adequate supply of fibre in the diet keeps your digestive system in good working order

fibre and bran

benefits

1 Help prevent constipation and other bowel problems.

2 Soluble fibre can help lower blood cholesterol levels.

drawback

Too much raw bran can interfere with mineral uptake and irritate the bowel.

Fibre – the indigestible cell walls of fruit, vegetables and cereals – contains no nutrients, yet is a vital part of a healthy diet. Its best-known function is to soak up water in the large intestine, making stools bulky, soft and easy to pass. The Department of Health recommends 18g of fibre a day, which is roughly equivalent to two slices of wholemeal bread, a bowl of muesli, a portion of broccoli and an apple. This should guard against constipation and may help reduce risks of bowel problems.

Fibre is found mainly in cereals, vegetables, fruit and pulses. Of the cereals, wholegrain varieties (such as wholemeal bread) are better sources than refined. This is because most fibre is contained in the outer layers of the grain, which is stripped out in the refining process.

There are two types of fibre: soluble and insoluble. Both help prevent constipation and other bowel disorders, but soluble fibre has two further benefits: it reduces blood cholesterol levels, by binding with cholesterol in the gut which then makes it easier for the body to excrete it; and it slows down glucose absorption, avoiding sudden, undesirable surges in blood sugar levels. You can easily increase your soluble fibre intake by eating oats and foods that contain them. For insoluble fibre eat processed bran products. Raw bran (the outer husk of wheat, rice or oats) is not recommended: it can irritate the intestine, causing wind and exacerbating certain digestive disorders (see DIGESTION). In addition, it contains phytic acid, which can hinder the absorption of zinc, calcium, iron and magnesium in the gut. Some foods, such as dried fruit and whole grains, are good sources of both soluble and insoluble fibre.

fibre providers

The main sources of fibre in our diet are vegetables, fruit, cereals and pulses. There are two types: soluble and insoluble. Certain foods are particularly rich in one or the other, while some foods are a good source of both.

SOLUBLE FIBRE
RELIEVES CONSTIPATION AND LOWERS BLOOD CHOLESTEROL
Oats, beans and peas.

INSOLUBLE FIBRE
HELPS PREVENT CONSTIPATION
Wholewheat, wheat bran, brown rice and nuts.

SOLUBLE AND INSOLUBLE FIBRE
REDUCE BLOOD CHOLESTEROL AND RISK OF BOWEL DISORDERS
Vegetables, whole grains, fruit and dried fruit.

Fish is packed with protein, and certain varieties can help to reduce the risks of heart disease and stroke

fish

Like meat, fish is a good source of protein, but unlike animal foods it is relatively low in calories and unhealthy fats. The healthiest way to prepare fish is to grill or bake it; frying adds unnecessary calories.

White fish is the low-fat choice but the fattier varieties can be good for you, too. Oil-rich fish – which includes salmon and trout (wild or farmed), mackerel, herring, sardines and fresh tuna – contains fats that actually promote health. These fats are known as omega-3 fatty acids, and ongoing research suggests they can reduce the risk of heart disease or stroke. They also appear to have anti-inflammatory properties, which may help to explain why eating oil-rich fish appears to relieve skin conditions such as psoriasis and dermatitis, as well as rheumatoid ARTHRITIS. (This benefit has also been attributed to the high vitamin D content of oil-rich fish.)

Omega-3 fatty acids are essential for healthy eyes and brain function, too – particularly in a developing foetus. Current nutritional guidelines suggest that pregnant women should try to include fresh tuna, mackerel, herring, sardines and

salmon in their diet. In addition, canned sardines eaten with their bones are an excellent source of calcium at all stages of life and especially for the formation of strong teeth and bones.

Always cook and eat oil-rich fish while it is fresh, as it deteriorates more quickly than white fish and can cause scombroid poisoning, resulting in an upset stomach and a rash. Unfortunately, canned tuna is no substitute for fresh as most of its oil content is removed in processing. However, other canned oil-rich fish retain their levels of omega-3 fatty acids. Smoking oil-rich fish to preserve it and give it a distinctive

eat more

Oil-rich fish, such as sardines, salmon, trout, mackerel and fresh tuna. Some nutritional experts suggest that everyone should aim to eat at least three portions a week.

eat less

Smoked, pickled and fried fish.

safety first

1 Fish can harbour parasitic worms, which may infect humans. Cook fish thoroughly, to destroy parasites and their eggs. Eating raw fish, as found in Japanese sushi dishes, carries a risk of infection.

2 Oil-rich fish that has been allowed to spoil may cause stomach upsets.

3 Fish bones can cause choking. Ensure that they are removed from fish served to children and elderly people.

flavour does not affect omega-3 fatty acid content or vitamin D levels. However, research has shown that the smoking process – like pickling – can produce carcinogenic compounds. So it's best to eat smoked and pickled fish in moderation.

White fish is much lower in fat than oil-rich fish: fat reserves are stored in the liver, leaving the flesh relatively fat-free and low in vitamins, except for B_{12} (essential for a healthy nervous system). The livers of cod and halibut are rich in vitamins A and D and are processed to extract their oil, a traditional food supplement. Two teaspoons of cod liver oil supply the adult daily requirement of vitamins A and D. The only good source of omega-3 fatty acids found in white fish is the roe of cod (used in the Greek dip taramasalata), but this is also high in cholesterol.

Flat fish – sole and plaice, for example – is similarly low in fat but high in protein and vitamin B_{12}. Other fresh fish such as swordfish, shark and skate have a firmer, 'meatier' flesh but are still low in fat.

Fish can be affected by pollution, and those with a long lifespan, such as tuna, can accumulate quite high concentrations of contaminants over many years. But the fishing industry is well aware of potential problems and all fish offered for sale is subject to strict monitoring procedures.

what's in fish?

type of fish	calories (kcal)	protein (g)	total fat (g)	omega-3 (g)	vit A (mcg)	vit D (mcg)	vit B_{12} (mcg)
COD (STEAMED)	83	18.6	0.9	0.3	2	trace	2
PLAICE (STEAMED)	93	18.9	1.9	0.1	trace	trace	2
MACKEREL (GRILLED)	239	20.8	17.3	2.0	48	5.4	1
CANNED SALMON	155	20.3	8.2	1.6	35	17	4.0
CANNED SARDINES	217	23.7	13.6	1.7	11	7.5	28

Nutrients per 100g (3½oz)

White fish is the low-fat choice but oil-rich fish – salmon,
fresh tuna and mackerel – contains fats that
can reduce heart disease risks.

If you use your common sense and follow basic rules of hygiene, the risk of food poisoning should be minimal

food poisoning

safety first

1 Be wary of undercooked poultry, raw or lightly cooked eggs, undercooked minced-beef products, unpasteurised dairy products, or rice kept warm for a long time.

2 Always follow basic hygiene rules when preparing and cooking your food.

3 Keep cold foods in the fridge and heat hot dishes thoroughly.

4 Store cooked and uncooked foods separately, to avoid cross-contamination.

5 Stuffing can harbour bacteria that has spread from raw poultry, because it rarely reaches a safe temperature inside the bird. It is safer to bake stuffing separately.

6 Abide by 'use by' dates on packaging. We cannot rely on our senses alone to tell us when food is off.

The usual sources of food poisoning are bacteria. Bacteria are literally everywhere, but most strains are harmless and those in yogurt are actually good for you. Relatively few types can cause sickness, and then only when they have multiplied to sufficiently large numbers. Supermarkets and other reputable food retailers and their suppliers all take great care to cut the risks of food poisoning. Some institutions and certain small independent food outlets have a less enviable reputation, but most outbreaks result from careless handling in the home.

When food poisoning does occur, it can be serious. Those particularly at risk are pregnant women, and the young, sick and elderly who may not have a strong immune system. This group should avoid raw or soft-cooked eggs, which can carry salmonella bacteria; and unpasteurised milk and cheeses and soft cheeses – such as Brie – which can carry listeria. (See chart, right.)

Good personal HYGIENE and PREPARING AND COOKING food in the right way greatly reduce the potential for food poisoning. For example, you should avoid leaving cooked foods at room temperature for too

bad bacteria

BACILLUS CEREUS
Typically found in rice that has been kept warm too long or has been insufficiently reheated. Causes vomiting within 1–4 hours or diarrhoea the next day. Sufferers usually recover quickly.

CAMPYLOBACTER JEJUNI
Most commonly carried in some raw poultry. Contamination often results from blood dripping on to cooked foods or salads. Causes fever, stomach pain, nausea and bloody diarrhoea. Symptoms appear within six days and last up to ten.

CLOSTRIDIUM BOTULINUM (BOTULISM)
A rare and deadly source of poisoning. Found in tinned or bottled meats, fish or vegetables that have not been sterilised thoroughly. Causes slurred speech, blurred vision, and respiratory problems within 18–36 hours.

ESCHERICHIA COLI (E. COLI)
A potentially deadly bacterium that has many strains. Common sources of infection are undercooked minced-beef products, notably beefburgers. Some strains cause vomiting and bloody diarrhoea within 12–72 hours, for up to ten days. Victims often need hospital treatment.

LISTERIA MONOCYTOGENES
Thrives in the intestines of many healthy people, causing no adverse effects. Found in soft cheeses (such as Brie) and unpasteurised milks. Breeds at fridge temperatures. May cause flu-like symptoms, within anything from four hours to several days. Dangerous for pregnant women, children and those with a weak immune system.

SALMONELLA
Most commonly found in raw or barely cooked eggs, undercooked poultry and cooked foods that are left unrefrigerated for several hours. Causes severe gastric upsets, fever and vomiting within 8–36 hours.

STAPHYLOCOCCUS AUREUS
Carried by many people and easily transferred to food. Usual sources are poultry, ham and cream. Causes stomach discomfort, vomiting, diarrhoea and occasionally chills and dizziness, within a few minutes to six hours.

long, especially in hot weather. A warm room provides the perfect temperature for bacteria to breed: keep all cold dishes in the refrigerator (at 0–5°C, 32–41°F) and serve hot dishes piping hot. Also, do not freeze or reheat food more than once.

Keep pets well away from kitchen worktops, as they can carry harmful bacteria. Remember to wash your hands after handling raw meat, to avoid spreading bacteria to food that will not be heated. Storing cooked and uncooked meat separately will also help to avoid cross-contamination. Some foods tend to be more vulnerable to bacterial infection than others. These include unpasteurised dairy products (pasteurisation destroys any harmful bacteria) and soft cheeses; raw eggs; uncooked or undercooked meat; shellfish obtained from suspect sources; and rice that has been kept warm for long periods.

If you do contract food poisoning, do not suppress the symptoms. Vomiting and diarrhoea are the body's natural way of expelling toxins. Do, however, drink plenty of water, to guard against dehydration.

frozen foods

Storing food at a very low temperature (–18°C/0°F is recommended) not only slows the enzyme action that makes food go off, it also suspends bacterial growth. Freezing does not kill bacteria: salmonella, for example, can survive low temperatures but it is destroyed by thorough cooking.

Foods suffer little nutrient loss during freezing. Some vitamin C is destroyed when vegetables are blanched (exposed to a high heat or dipped into boiling water) before they are frozen, but the loss is not significant. Blanching can also reduce thiamin, which the body needs to unlock energy from food; and folate, necessary to guard against spina bifida in pregnancy. But some foods are actually enhanced by freezing: when peas, for example, are frozen within hours of picking, their natural sugar content is prevented from turning into starch.

Pre-prepared frozen foods all carry 'best before' dates because prolonged freezing causes the food's structure to break down, spoiling its texture. As a general rule, eat meat and fish within three to six months, fruit within nine and vegetables within 12.

safety first

To avoid any risk of food poisoning from frozen foods:

1 **Keep your freezer at –18°C (0°F).**

2 **Thaw foods in the fridge or in the microwave. Do not try to defrost food by heating it in the oven.**

3 **Never refreeze foods once they have thawed.**

gallstones

eat more

1 Rice, bread and other starchy foods.

2 Fresh fruit and vegetables for fibre.

3 Pulses (peas, beans, lentils) and oats for soluble fibre.

4 Globe artichokes.

cut down on

1 Refined foods.

2 Red meat.

3 Fried and fatty foods.

A build-up of crystals of cholesterol, calcium or bile pigments can form hard lumps or 'stones' in the gallbladder or bile duct. Symptoms range from mild discomfort in the upper abdomen to severe pain with vomiting, in which case surgery may be needed to remove the stones. Gallstones are more common in women than in men; sufferers tend to be over 40 and overweight, but other people can be afflicted, too.

A low-fat, high-fibre diet can help prevent existing stones enlarging, assist the passage of small stones that are excreted into the gut, and discourage new ones from forming. People with gallstones should eat more starchy carbohydrates and fresh fruit and vegetables; cut down on refined foods, red meat and high-fat foods; and drink plenty of fluids. Foods high in soluble fibre can lower blood cholesterol levels, reducing the likelihood of gallstones. Some studies suggest that cynarin, found in globe artichokes, may also help prevent gallstones.

garlic

benefits

1 Helps to fight infection – from flu to a stomach bug.

2 May lower blood pressure and blood cholesterol levels.

drawbacks

1 Makes breath smell. Eating parsley is the traditional antidote.

2 May cause migraines, allergies or contact dermatitis in susceptible people.

The Ancient Greeks valued garlic as a food, and naturopaths have long used it to treat a huge range of complaints. More recently, scientific evidence has confirmed its therapeutic benefits.

Garlic contains sulphur compounds, which account for both its pungent smell and its medicinal properties. Raw garlic has greater health benefits than cooked. Studies have shown that it helps to prevent and subdue bacterial and viral infections, from gastroenteritis to the common cold. Other studies confirm that garlic is good for the heart. Eating just two cloves a day can lower blood cholesterol levels by 10 per cent and reduce blood pressure. Larger amounts – ten cloves a day – inhibit blood clotting (which may help to prevent a heart attack) and reduce the risk of thrombosis. A study in China suggests garlic may also help reduce risks of stomach cancer.

gastritis

In both the acute and chronic forms of gastritis, the stomach lining becomes inflamed. Symptoms include stomach pain, indigestion or heartburn and nausea. In long-term cases, the stomach walls produce so little digestive acid that vitamin B_{12} absorption is inhibited and there is a risk of ANAEMIA. Prolonged damage to the stomach lining may also lead to ULCERS.

Likely causes of gastritis include excessive intakes of alcohol, strong coffee or tea, highly spiced or fried foods, and aspirins. Anyone suffering from gastritis should cut right down on all these. Stress is another possible trigger, as is a gut infection that is caused by the bacterium *Helicobacter pylori* (which can also give rise to gastric ulcers). Among elderly people there can sometimes be a link between anti-arthritis drugs and chronic bouts of gastritis.

A regime of regular, frequent, small meals of bland foods that are gentle on the stomach should help to ease most of the symptoms. And many gastritis sufferers find they also gain at least some relief by drinking plenty of camomile tea.

eat more

Small meals at frequent intervals.

cut down on

1 Alcohol.

2 Strong tea and coffee.

3 Highly spiced foods.

4 Fried foods.

gastroenteritis

Although popularly known as 'traveller's tummy', this inflammation of the stomach and intestines is just as likely to occur at home as abroad. Gastroenteritis is usually due to infection by viruses or the bacteria that trigger FOOD POISONING. Common causes are poor hygiene, careless storage or cooking, and disregard for 'best before' dates. Symptoms include acute diarrhoea, vomiting, stomach cramps and mild fever, and may last from a few hours to five days. To begin with, drink only fluids – plenty of water mixed with rehydration solutions, or fruit juice diluted 50:50 with water. When the symptoms have subsided a diet of bananas, boiled rice, apples and toast (the 'BRAT' diet) can help to ease you back on to other foods. Bananas are rich in potassium, which helps to regulate the body's fluid levels; rice and white toast offer carbohydrate for energy; apples help cleanse the digestive system and their pectin helps to treat diarrhoea. Eat small amounts of each food at regular intervals for 48 hours, then slowly introduce your usual foods and gradually return to your normal diet.

drink more

Water and rehydration solutions to replace lost fluids.

eat more

1 Bananas for potassium.

2 Boiled white rice and dry white toast for low-fibre carbohydrate.

3 Apples to cleanse the digestive system.

They have many potential benefits, but there are some unanswered questions about genetically modified foods

gm foods

benefits

1 **Longer shelf-life for fresh produce.**

2 **Improved nutritional value, flavour or visual appeal.**

3 **Pest-resistant crops leading to higher yields and lower costs.**

4 **Hardy crops that will grow in most soils and climates.**

drawback

A lack of certainty about the long-term effects of all GM foods on our health and environment.

By the targeting of specific genes, genetic modification (GM) allows features of one plant or animal to be combined more easily with another. It enables farmers to produce pest-resistant crops, increasing yields. It may also have the potential to boost the nutritional value of crops – for example, by adding a gene to make oil seed rape produce more unsaturated fatty acids or by increasing the vitamin A content of rice to help prevent blindness in Asia. So ultimately, GM ingredients could provide better value and even improve our health.

GM is also being used to develop crops that thrive in hostile environments, such as deserts and cold climates, with obvious potential to ease world food shortages.

However, GM is a young science and, as in any field of rapid technological development, there are many uncertainties about its long-term impact. Although the government's Chief Medical Officer and Chief Scientific Adviser stated in their 1999 report that there was no evidence that GM foods posed any risks to human health, they also recommended further research and close monitoring of developments. The British public, however, remains wary. While some people have ethical reservations about scientists meddling with nature, others are nervous that GM technology may be storing up possible health problems for the future.

Some wildlife experts are anxious about the unknown dangers of GM foods to the environment. There is a worry, for example, that insect-resistant crops could lead to the extinction of certain insect species (such as ladybirds), reducing the biodiversity of the planet. Although all GM crop trials in this country are closely monitored, concerns about the long-term implications of large-scale GM cultivation remain.

In response to consumer concern, some supermarkets have decided to remove GM ingredients from their own-label products. By law, any genetically modified soya or maize in foods must be clearly identified on food labels. And since September 1999, restaurants, cafés and sandwich shops have been required to notify customers about GM ingredients, via their staff or menus. So anyone wanting to avoid GM foods should read food labels or consult retailers.

gooseberries

Even the sweeter varieties of gooseberry retain a characteristic sharpness and are rarely eaten raw. Some of their vitamin C content is lost in cooking, but a typical 100g (3½oz) portion of stewed fruit still contains more than a quarter of the adult daily requirement. Gooseberries also contain potassium (helps maintain normal blood pressure) and fibre (needed for efficient digestion). Although low in calories, they are unlikely candidates for a slimming diet because they are usually stewed with sugar and often eaten with cream.

benefits

1 Useful source of vitamin C.

2 Contain potassium.

3 Useful source of soluble fibre.

gout

Contrary to popular belief, this form of arthritis is not caused by overindulging in food and drink – though this may trigger an attack. The underlying cause of the condition is a defect in metabolism, which leads to a build-up of acid crystals in the joints, causing painful inflammation.

More men than women suffer from gout, which is often hereditary. It is also associated with aging and not drinking enough water. It is treated with drugs to speed uric acid excretion and to ease inflammation. But diet can help, too. Anyone with gout should avoid high-purine foods – poultry and shellfish – which raise uric acid levels; low-purine foods include dairy products, fruit and vegetables (but not cauliflower, peas, spinach or mushrooms). Drink plenty of fluids to help dissolve uric acid crystals and discourage their formation, and eat potassium-rich fruit and vegetables to help uric acid excretion. Studies show that fish-oil supplements with omega-3 fatty acids may relieve pain, and CHERRIES can help lower uric acid levels. Herbalists claim that celery has an anti-inflammatory effect.

eat more

1 Fresh fruit and vegetables.

2 Low-purine foods (nuts, dairy products, fruit and vegetables).

drink more

Water and other non-alcoholic drinks.

avoid

1 Too much alcohol.

2 High-purine foods (offal, game, poultry, sardines and shellfish).

grapefruit

benefits

1 Rich source of vitamin C, vital for a healthy immune system.

2 Contain pectin, which helps to lower blood cholesterol levels.

3 Contain potassium, which helps to regulate blood pressure.

Together with the other members of the citrus-fruit family, grapefruit are rich in vitamin C, which helps our bodies fight off infection. Just half a grapefruit provides more than 50 per cent of the adult daily requirement of the vitamin. Grapefruit also contain bioflavonoids, substances that scientists suspect may help to protect against certain forms of cancer.

A grapefruit's nutritional value is not only in its juicy flesh: both the membranes between the segments and the white pith contain pectin, a soluble fibre that can help to reduce blood cholesterol levels. So to derive the maximum nutritional benefits, eat the whole peeled fruit.

The potassium in grapefruit helps to maintain healthy blood pressure and a regular heartbeat. Low in calories – unless you add a lot of sugar – and virtually fat-free, grapefruit are a favourite among those on a low-fat diet. Pink grapefruit are slightly higher in vitamin C than the yellow varieties, and also contain beta carotene, which the body converts to vitamin A (essential for growth, vision and immune function).

grapes and raisins

benefits

1 Useful sources of potassium.

2 Contain bioflavonoids, which may protect against certain cancers.

3 Calorie-packed raisins are a good source of energy for athletes.

drawbacks

1 May trigger migraines in some people.

2 Sugar-rich raisins can encourage tooth decay.

Sweet, juicy grapes (particularly seedless varieties) are a favourite food for convalescents. Light and easy to eat, they lack the acidity of many other fruits. And despite their sweetness, a 100g (3½oz) portion contains only about 60 Calories. Grapes also provide potassium, which helps to regulate the body's fluid levels and blood pressure, as well as small amounts of other essential minerals and vitamins.

Both red and black grapes contain bioflavonoids – antioxidants that may protect the body against certain cancers. On the down side, the tannins and polyphenols in red grapes occasionally trigger migraines in susceptible people, and there is a risk of pesticide residues on grape skins, so be sure to wash them thoroughly.

Raisins, or dried grapes, are a concentrated source of calories: their high natural sugar content (more than four times that of grapes) makes them an ideal high-energy snack for anyone doing a lot of physical exercise. In addition, a handful (50g/2oz) provides about 15 per cent of the adult daily requirement of potassium.

Half a grapefruit supplies more than half the adult daily requirement of vitamin C.

hair and scalp problems

eat more

1 Shellfish, red meat, pumpkin seeds and Brazil nuts, to boost zinc intake and help relieve a dry scalp.

2 Foods containing B vitamins, such as meat and dairy products.

3 Oil-rich fish, nuts and vegetable oils for their essential fatty acids.

4 Liver (except during pregnancy) and eggs for extra vitamin A.

Hair and scalp problems often arise when you are feeling a bit under the weather, or you are stressed. People under severe stress may be deficient in B vitamins, which can cause anything from dull, lifeless hair to significant hair loss. In these cases the daily diet should include more eggs, yogurt, milk, oil-rich fish, yeast extract, peas and wholegrain cereals.

Vegetarians and vegans may be prone to dry skin and dandruff because their diet supplies insufficient zinc (found mainly in red meat and shellfish); eating pumpkin seeds and cashew and Brazil nuts may help to redress the imbalance. Essential fatty acids (found in most vegetable oils and oil-rich fish such as sardines and salmon) may also relieve a dry scalp – even in sufferers of the skin condition psoriasis.

Research shows that too little vitamin A may lead to lacklustre hair. Liver is a particularly rich source of the vitamin, so including more liver in your diet (but not if you are pregnant) and eggs – another good source of vitamin A – may help hair to regain its shine and vitality.

hay diet

food note

Useful aspects of the Hay diet include eating more fruit and vegetables, and cutting down on fats. However, few nutritionists accept its basic principle of not eating proteins and carbohydrates in the same meal.

The Hay diet was developed by an American doctor at the beginning of the 20th century and is based on the discovery that protein-containing foods are digested by enzymes under acidic conditions, while enzymes that break down carbohydrates need alkaline conditions.

Dr William Hay's theory was that as the two food types need different conditions for effective digestion, they should not be eaten together in the same meal or even within four hours of each other. This idea has been largely discredited by nutritionists today, as we now appreciate that the body digests proteins and carbohydrates at different stages: proteins are broken down in the acidic juices of the stomach while carbohydrates are digested further along in the small intestine.

However, other principles of the Hay diet are in line with current thinking on healthy eating: plenty of fruit and vegetables, and a limited intake of fats. It is still not fully understood why those who follow this diet often lose weight – it may simply be that they think about their diet more carefully.

Recurring headaches – even migraines – can sometimes be prevented by simple changes in diet

headaches

A headache can take many different forms – from a dull pressure in the temples to an intense, throbbing pain that radiates over the entire skull. When the discomfort is centred behind one eye and – in some instances – preceded or accompanied by visual disturbances and nausea, it is generally termed a migraine.

Research indicates that headaches – of all kinds – can be triggered by many different influences, including tension, eye strain, nasal congestion, poor posture, high blood pressure and hormonal fluctuations. There are also several diet-related causes that are worth investigating.

Skipping meals, which is known to cause blood sugar to plummet, can precipitate a headache. Try eating regular, light meals – and if you often wake with a headache, have a small starchy snack before bedtime to prevent your blood sugar levels from falling too low overnight.

Dehydration is another common source of headaches, particularly in hot weather or following strenuous exercise. A few extra glasses of water will help. A hangover headache is usually due to dehydration.

Too much caffeine – in tea and coffee, for example – can also give you a headache, by altering blood supply to the brain. If you think you need to cut down, phase it out gradually, otherwise you are likely to suffer withdrawal headaches.

Certain headaches, in particular migraines, can be sparked by specific foods. The chief culprits are usually cheese, chocolate, citrus fruits and red wine. Keeping a daily food diary, and cutting out suspect foods one by one, can help identify a trigger food. Food ALLERGIES have also been known to cause headaches.

Doctors sometimes recommend a chiropractor, osteopath or cranial osteopath, to realign bones in the neck and skull that could be causing regular headaches. Herbalists will often prescribe the herb feverfew to treat migraines. It is available in tablet form and, taken regularly, is said to reduce the frequency of attacks.

Headaches are rarely the symptom of a serious underlying disorder. However, you should seek expert medical attention as soon as possible if you suddenly start to experience persistent, severe headaches.

eat more

Regular, light meals – and try eating a small starchy snack last thing at night.

cut down on

1 **Alcohol.**

2 **Tea and coffee – but be sure to phase them out gradually.**

drink more

Water.

A diet low in saturated fat and high in fruit and vegetables will help keep your heart healthy

heart disease

eat more

1 Red, orange and green fruits and vegetables for antioxidants.

2 Oats and pulses for soluble fibre.

3 Oil-rich fish for omega-3 fatty acids.

4 Garlic to reduce blood cholesterol.

5 Pulses and green vegetables for B vitamins.

cut down on

1 Fatty red meats.

2 Butter, cream and high-fat cheeses.

3 Salty and smoked foods.

avoid

1 Smoking.

2 Too much alcohol, which can raise blood pressure.

Despite significant medical advances in recent years, coronary heart disease is still the single largest killer in the UK. Eating a healthy diet is one of the most effective ways to protect yourself against it.

How the heart works

The heart is a muscular organ that pumps oxygen-rich blood round the body via the arteries, nourishing every cell. From childhood onwards, these arteries, or blood vessels, can start to accumulate plaque (cholesterol and other fatty deposits). This process is called atherosclerosis, or 'furring up' of the arteries, and tends to develop over a period of 20 to 30 years. Eventually, the build-up of plaque can clog the arteries, restricting the flow of oxygenated blood. When atherosclerosis develops in the arteries that supply the brain, a stroke can result. When it affects the arteries that supply the heart itself (coronary arteries), it can cause chronic chest pain (angina), irregular heartbeat (arrhythmia) and – ultimately – a heart attack.

Angina can be one of the first signs of heart disease. It is caused by a partially blocked coronary artery. It often strikes when the heart is working harder than

case study

Since his father had high blood cholesterol levels, Simon, aged 25, was advised to have a cholesterol test. A non-smoker and a moderate drinker with a fairly active lifestyle, Simon's weight was normal, but his blood cholesterol level was found to be on the high side. His GP suggested a change of diet. He was advised to cut down on fatty meats, full-fat cheese, full-cream milk and fried foods, and to eat more lean meat, poultry, fish, vegetables, fruit, cereals, rice and pasta. Six months later Simon's cholesterol levels were normal, but his GP told him to stick to his new diet to prevent them rising again.

usual, during a period of physical activity, or mental stress for example. It is thought to affect two million Britons each year.

Over time, a coronary artery may become totally blocked, either by further build-up of plaque or by a blood clot (thrombosis), or both. This starves the heart muscle of oxygenated blood, triggering a heart attack. A heart attack may be mild, if only a small amount of muscle is damaged, or fatal if a large percentage dies. Bypass surgery can drastically reduce the risk of heart attack in those with furred coronary arteries, by creating a detour (using a healthy vein or artery) around a blockage.

The major risk factors

Risk factors fall into two categories: those you can do something about and those you cannot. Those factors outside your control are gender, age and family history. Men are more susceptible to heart problems than women, and in both men and women the risk rises with age (especially in post-menopausal women). Heart disease tends to run in families: if you have a parent or sibling who has had a heart attack, you are more likely to develop cardiac disorders.

Chief among the factors that you can influence are blood CHOLESTEROL levels. Blood cholesterol is the fat-like, waxy substance produced by the liver for various vital functions in the body. (It should not be confused with dietary cholesterol, which is present in foods like cream and red meat.) High levels of blood cholesterol can increase the risk of fatty deposits building up in the arteries and causing heart problems. Recent figures suggest that a third of men and a third of women in the UK have unhealthy levels of blood cholesterol. In some instances, high levels can be inherited, but they are also determined by intake of saturated fat (found predominantly in fatty meats and full-fat dairy products).

High BLOOD PRESSURE, or hypertension, can make you more vulnerable to heart problems. This condition develops when

Some studies have shown that one to two units of alcohol a day may help protect against heart disease in men over 40 and post-menopausal women.

food note

You do not have to forgo all your favourite foods to reduce your risk of heart disease: just replace them with more heart-healthy varieties. Then when you do have the odd cream cake, you need not worry.

1 **Use vegetable oils (such as olive oil) in place of butter and margarine.**

2 **Eat skinless poultry in preference to fatty red meats.**

3 **Substitute low-salt bacon for your regular variety.**

4 **Choose low-fat fromage frais or yogurt rather than cream.**

5 **Opt for reduced- or low-fat cheese instead of full-fat varieties.**

the arterioles (small blood vessels) lose their ability to relax naturally, increasing resistance to blood flow and forcing the heart to work harder. When combined with high blood cholesterol levels, high blood pressure can speed up atherosclerosis. Everyone has a higher than average blood pressure at certain times – for example, after running up stairs – but when blood pressure consistently registers above the normal levels action needs to be taken.

Too much salt and ALCOHOL can also raise blood pressure. Research has shown that heavy drinkers – men who consume over 50 units a week and women who have more than 35 – are twice as likely to die of heart disease as non-drinkers. A unit is equivalent to a small (125ml) glass of wine, a half-pint of beer or one measure of spirits.

STRESS is often cited as a risk factor for heart disease. When we are under pressure, the stress hormone adrenaline stimulates

Regular exercise can help fend off heart disease. It can lower blood cholesterol and blood pressure. As little as 20 to 30 minutes walking a day can make a difference.

Smoking is another significant risk factor for heart disease. Nicotine stimulates the production of adrenaline, increasing the heart rate as well as blood pressure. And certain chemicals in cigarette smoke can damage the arteries and may also increase the likelihood of blood clots. Smoking accounts for one in five of all deaths from heart disease. But smokers who quit will halve their risk within just one year.

Obesity also increases the risk of heart disease, since it can lead to both high blood cholesterol levels and high blood pressure.

the release of fatty acids and glucose into the bloodstream. This is designed to fuel muscles for the so-called 'fight or flight' response, but it can also increase levels of blood cholesterol. In the long term this could raise the risk of heart disease.

Strategies to reduce the risks

The fact that Britain has one of the highest rates of heart disease in the world is largely attributed to our diet. The typical British diet tends to include too much saturated fat (found in foods such as butter and cheese), which increases blood cholesterol levels and leads to furring of the arteries. Replacing some of these FATS with unsaturated fats (monounsaturates such as olive oil and polyunsaturates such as sunflower oil) can help keep cholesterol in check. Fish oils, such as the polyunsaturated oil found in salmon and sardines, are particularly recommended: they are rich in omega-3 fatty acids, which may reduce the risk of blood clots. Nutritionists recommend eating three portions of oil-rich fish a week because of its beneficial effect on the heart.

Foods rich in soluble FIBRE, such as oats, beans and lentils, may help reduce blood cholesterol levels. The fibre binds with cholesterol in the gut, making it easier for the body to excrete it. Including garlic in your diet is said to reduce blood cholesterol, too.

Nutritional experts have long recognised that a high intake of ANTIOXIDANTS, found in most fruit and vegetables, may help keep your heart healthy. Antioxidants such as beta carotene and vitamins C and E help to prevent cholesterol from oxidising and furring up the arteries. Five portions of fresh fruit and vegetables a day is the minimum recommended intake.

The very latest scientific research suggests that an adequate intake of B vitamins is crucial to prevent heart disease. If your diet is deficient in vitamins B_6, B_{12} and folic acid, your blood levels of the amino acid homocysteine, which the body makes from protein-rich foods, may rise, and this could speed up atherosclerosis. Vitamin B-rich foods include pulses and green vegetables.

Some studies have shown that one to two units of alcohol a day may help to protect against heart disease in men over 40 and post-menopausal women. Alcohol boosts blood flow by dilating small blood vessels. It also raises levels of high density lipoproteins – molecules that transport cholesterol out of the body. Too much alcohol, however, increases blood pressure and raises the risk of heart disease.

Aside from medication, other measures to cut your risk of heart disease include exercise and stress reduction. Regular aerobic exercise can lower blood cholesterol and blood pressure, increase the flow of oxygen-rich blood to the heart, strengthen the heart muscle and reduce weight. As little as 20 to 30 minutes walking a day can help. Exercise can also reduce stress, burning off the stress hormone adrenaline, which can increase blood cholesterol. It may be worth investigating other stress-reduction techniques, such as meditation, yoga, massage and aromatherapy.

health note

During their reproductive years, women are less vulnerable to heart attacks than men. This is because the hormone oestrogen keeps their cholesterol levels in check. But after the menopause, when oestrogen levels drop, women's cholesterol levels rise, making them much more prone to heart disease. Hormone Replacement Therapy (HRT) offers some protection, by restoring lost oestrogen. However, HRT does not suit all women because it can sometimes cause unpleasant side effects.

Herbal infusions can help to ease a variety of everyday ailments – from indigestion to insomnia

herbs

try

1 Mint or fennel teas to help digestion.

2 Elderflower tea to ward off a cold.

3 Camomile tea to relax and get a good night's sleep.

avoid

Raspberry leaf tea in the early stages of pregnancy: it can cause miscarriage.

Although they are a great way to liven up a meal, herbs are unlikely to add significant nutritional value to a diet, as they are normally used in too small a quantity to have any effect. Many herbs that we cook with have been used for centuries for medicinal purposes, too. However, herbal medicine is a controversial subject. Many Western doctors and scientists are reluctant to consider herbal remedies as an adjunct or alternative to conventional drugs – even though many drugs were derived from plant extracts before being synthesised in a laboratory. And although practitioners of Chinese and Indian herbal medicine are highly regarded within their communities, they often meet with suspicion outside as their treatments are not understood.

While you should not try to treat serious medical problems using herbs yourself, plenty of minor ailments and discomforts can be eased by simple herbal infusions that have been used here for centuries as home remedies without posing any risks.

Indigestion, for example, can often be helped by a glass of mint tea, either made Moroccan style, with boiling water poured over a handful of leaves in a glass, or with pre-packaged teabags. Fennel tea, if drunk after indulging in a heavy meal, also assists digestion and dispels wind.

Camomile tea has a relaxing effect, and if drunk before bedtime it can encourage a good night's sleep. Hot elderflower is an old country remedy given at the first sign of a cold: use teabags or brew your own infusions from the flowers. Raspberry leaf tea, if drunk regularly during the final 12 weeks of pregnancy, is said to make labour and delivery easier. But never drink it in early pregnancy: it can cause a miscarriage.

A glass of mint or peppermint tea helps digestion, especially if taken after a rich meal.

hives

Also known as nettle rash or urticaria, hives is a rash of itchy red or white raised patches that can occur anywhere on the body. It is caused by the chemical histamine being released into the bloodstream as part of an allergic reaction.

Any number of triggers can cause the reaction. Animal hair is a common culprit, and in some people hives can be brought on by insect bites or an allergy to aspirin or penicillin; in others, food ALLERGIES are to blame. Strawberries, shellfish, beans, celery, milk, onions and garlic, nuts, spices and the food colouring tartrazine (E102) have all been implicated. Exposure to sunlight while eating specific trigger foods can exacerbate the reaction, while eating foods rich in beta carotene may help relieve the condition when it is affected by sunlight.

The B vitamin niacin is thought to inhibit histamine production, so when you have a rash, try to eat more meat, pulses, offal or wheatgerm, which are all good sources.

In the majority of cases hives disappears after about three days but it can be treated with antihistamine if necessary.

eat more

1 Meat, pulses, offal and wheatgerm, which contain niacin.

2 Orange and yellow fruit and vegetables, plus dark leafy green vegetables, for beta carotene, if sunlight makes your hives worse.

avoid

Any foods to which you know you are susceptible.

honey

Many extravagant claims have been made over the centuries about honey's beneficial properties, but little has been proved.

It is essentially a mixture of two sugars – fructose and glucose – in water. But honey also contains minute traces of other nutrients, and is a useful source of chromium, a vital link in the chain that makes glucose available to the body. Honey has fewer calories than sugar because of its water content: 100g (3½oz) honey contains 288 Calories; 100g (3½oz) sugar has 394. But you cannot substitute honey for sugar in order to cut calories: honey is denser than sugar, so a spoonful weighs more than a spoonful of sugar and has more calories.

Just as there are standards for olive oil, so there are for honey. Cold-pressed is the top quality: other honey may have been heated or filtered, destroying or removing delicate components. (In time all runny honey will become thick and granular. Warming it restores its texture.) Some naturopaths claim that pollen traces in cold-pressed honey may help desensitise hay fever sufferers if they take a teaspoon or two a day.

try

A traditional remedy: drink honey and hot water with lemon to ease a sore throat.

avoid

Giving honey to babies under one year: there is a real risk of food poisoning because of the presence of bacterial spores.

hygiene

always

1 Keep raw meat and fish on the lowest shelf of the fridge.

2 Defrost freezers and fridges regularly to keep them working properly.

never

1 Put warm foods in the fridge or freezer, as they will warm it up.

2 Chop raw foods with a knife then use it to cut cooked food without first washing it up.

All food comes into contact with bacteria – they are present everywhere – but they only become a problem when they multiply in numbers likely to affect our health. Following the basic rules of good hygiene limits opportunities for bacteria to breed and prevents cross-contamination of foods.

Bacteria thrive in warm, moist conditions. Keeping worktops and chopping boards clean and dry, and boiling dishcloths before hanging them on the washing line, deprives bacteria of two favourite breeding sites. Some foods are more likely than others to carry bacteria. For example, raw chicken may harbour salmonella, which is destroyed by cooking at high temperatures. However, if juices drip from raw chicken on to a lettuce, say, there is a risk of FOOD POISONING as the lettuce will be served uncooked. So a separate chopping board should be kept for cutting raw meat.

People carry bacteria, too. Always wash your hands before you prepare food; if you need to blow your nose or visit the toilet, you will have to wash them again. And keep pets away from kitchen worktops.

hyperactivity

avoid

1 Giving children tea, coffee and cola drinks, and ration chocolate bars, as they all contain caffeine.

2 Foods and drinks containing food colourings such as tartrazine (E102) and preservatives such as benzoic acid.

Parents may complain their children are hyperactive when they really mean overactive, as true hyperactivity is fortunately quite rare. There is still some controversy as to whether hyperactivity and diet are linked, but studies on children with behavioural problems have shown that they improved when certain ADDITIVES and caffeine were cut from their diet. Evidence suggests that the food colouring tartrazine (E102), often used in orange squash, may affect some children, as may benzoic acid. Caffeine, a strong stimulant in tea and coffee, is also in most cola-type drinks and chocolate bars. Salicylates, naturally occurring aspirin-like compounds, have also been implicated in some research. They are present in most fruits, broccoli, carrots, spinach and potato skins. But consult a doctor before modifying your child's diet or you may cut out vital nutrients.

Overactive, rather than hyperactive, children may respond to a daily routine that includes plenty of exercise and periods when they get a parent's full attention. Avoiding stressful situations can help, too.

Almost everyone loves ice cream. It can be part of a balanced diet – but do check the fat and sugar content

ice cream

Whether in a cone or a tub, on a stick or in a family-size container, ice cream appeals to all ages. The quality, variety and range of flavours has never been greater. Traditional ingredients such as cream are back in favour. And many chocolate bars are now available in frozen form.

Ice creams have good nutritional value; they all supply protein, calcium for strong bones, and vitamins A, B_2 (riboflavin) and B_{12}. But, depending on the cream content, they can be high in saturated fat. Other ingredients include sugar and flavourings; stabilisers and emulsifiers are often added to improve consistency and durability.

The fat content of ice cream ranges from 5 to 15 per cent. Anything that contains less than 5 per cent must be called 'frozen dessert'. A 'dairy ice cream' is made with milk fat: if other fats are used, the label must state 'contains non-milk fat' or 'contains vegetable fat'.

Both dairy and non-dairy ice creams are high in saturated fats, which have been linked with heart disease. The Department of Health recommends that no more than 10 per cent of our total daily calorie intake should come from saturated fats. So while ice creams can be part of a healthy diet, eat them in moderation or try to choose those with a relatively low fat content.

Frozen plain low-fat yogurt is a tempting alternative to dairy ice cream for weight-watchers. Even creamy yogurts contain just 5–7 per cent fat – only slightly more than whole milk but much less than cream. Yogurt supplies calcium and phosphorus for strong bones and teeth, as well as vitamins B_2 (riboflavin) and B_{12}. Children often prefer frozen fruit yogurts to ice cream, but these do tend to contain a large amount of sugar – about 15 per cent.

Sorbets, or water ices, are fat-free but higher in calories than you might imagine because of their sugar content. An average serving of lemon sorbet, for example, has 124 Calories compared with 146 Calories for an equivalent serving of dairy vanilla ice cream. Depending on the fruit flavouring, sorbets supply varying amounts of vitamins and minerals. Frozen chocolate confectionery is high in fat and calories: a frozen chocolate bar might contain 17–21g of fat and 260–300 Calories.

benefits

1 **Contains calcium.**

2 **Most types contain vitamins A, B_2 (riboflavin) and B_{12}.**

drawbacks

1 **Most types are high in saturated fat.**

2 **Many have a high sugar content.**

A nutrient-rich diet will help to maintain and boost your body's defences against infection and disease

immune system

eat more

1 Zinc-rich foods, such as oysters and other shellfish, meat, nuts, sunflower seeds and pumpkin seeds.

2 Citrus fruits and potatoes for vitamin C.

3 Vegetable oils for vitamin E.

4 Carrots and green leafy vegetables for vitamin A.

5 Foods that contain selenium, such as offal, meat, fish, wholegrain cereals and Brazil nuts.

avoid

1 Too much alcohol and caffeine.

2 High stress.

The body's natural defence system, the immune system, is designed to fight off infections and diseases. Its guardians are different types of white blood cells, which destroy harmful micro-organisms. Hostile invaders are identified by their chemical characteristics (antigens), then antibodies are produced to attack and destroy them. Antibodies recognise and respond to specific aggressors; and once formed they will protect us from getting certain diseases again. Occasionally, substances that are completely harmless in themselves, such as pollen or certain foods, are perceived by the body as hostile invaders: the immune system overreacts inappropriately, and this is what causes ALLERGIES.

While a diet rich in vitamins and minerals helps to maintain a healthy immune system, certain foods are especially valuable in boosting the body's defences, whether against the common cold or cancer.

Zinc is vital to the immune system. Even a mild deficiency of the mineral increases the risk of infection. Elderly people, who tend to be more vulnerable to infection, should be particularly careful to include plenty of zinc-rich foods in their daily diet: oysters and other shellfish, meat, peanuts, and pumpkin seeds are good sources.

Foods rich in ANTIOXIDANT vitamins A, C and E and selenium can all help boost the body's natural resistance to disease. They can also help to neutralise free radicals, chemicals that form part of the body's defence armoury but which, in excess, can actually increase the risk of disease.

Lemons, grapefruit and blackcurrants provide bioflavonoids, which help ward off cancers; and both garlic and broccoli contain cancer-inhibiting compounds. Garlic, onion and cranberries are antibacterial, as is live YOGURT, which encourages friendly bacteria in the gut that help resist illness.

A healthy lifestyle lightens the load on the immune system. Always maintain high standards of hygiene to reduce the chance of harmful micro-organisms entering the body. As stress puts strain on the immune system, counter it with yoga, meditation and deep-breathing exercises. Try to get enough sleep: tiredness weakens resistance to illness. And avoid too much alcohol or caffeine, which reduce immune capability.

impotence

The causes of a man's inability to have or maintain an erection may be physical or psychological. Physical disorders that can lead to impotence include DIABETES, atherosclerosis and any ailments that affect the nervous system, urinary tract and genitals. High stress levels and tiredness can also cause impotence – as can anxiety, guilt, embarrassment or depression.

Whatever the cause, alcohol, caffeine and nicotine are likely to make the situation worse. Alcohol can weaken nerve signals and, in excess, it may suppress production of male hormones (androgens). Caffeine and nicotine both constrict blood vessels, thereby restricting blood flow.

A zinc deficiency can also be a cause of impotence; recent research shows that zinc supplements improve potency and raise levels of the male sex hormone (testosterone). Oysters (said to be an aphrodisiac) are an excellent dietary source of zinc.

A recent study suggests a link between high blood cholesterol levels and an increased long-term risk of impotence. So a diet low in saturated fats is advisable.

eat more

Foods rich in zinc, such as seafood (especially shellfish), lean meat, offal, lentils, nuts, and both sunflower and pumpkin seeds.

cut down on

1 **Alcohol.**

2 **Caffeine – in coffee, tea and cola drinks.**

3 **Smoking.**

infertility

Failure to conceive is a fairly common problem. It can be caused by a range of medical problems in either partner, and the risk of infertility in men or women can also be increased by poor nutrition.

Obesity or excessive dieting can reduce a woman's chances of conception. If the level of body fat drops below the optimum 18 per cent of body weight, hormone imbalances can occur that may result in failure to ovulate. A woman who wants to conceive should ensure her diet provides zinc, magnesium, iron, folate, vitamin C and essential fatty acids (found in oil-rich fish and polyunsaturated oils). Coming off the Pill after many years can reduce fertility for a while – maybe months: a diet of foods rich in vitamins and minerals will help to restore a normal hormonal balance.

A man's diet should include essential fatty acids; vitamins A, B, C and E; and zinc and selenium: all encourage healthy sperm production.

Avoid too much alcohol (which depletes the body's B vitamins and certain minerals), and tea, which inhibits uptake of iron.

eat more

1 **Shellfish, lean meat, nuts, sunflower and pumpkin seeds for zinc.**

2 **Citrus fruits and kiwi fruit for vitamin C.**

3 **Lean meat and offal for iron.**

cut down on

1 **Alcohol.**

2 **Tea, which reduces absorption of iron.**

Many people suffer from this condition for years. But plenty of water, fruit and vegetables could help cure it

irritable bowel syndrome

eat more

1 **Fresh fruit, vegetables and oat-based cereals, for soluble fibre.**

2 **Live yogurt, for its friendly bacteria.**

avoid

1 **Foods that tend to produce wind, such as beans, lentils and peas.**

2 **Bran and high-fibre breakfast cereals that contain wheat bran.**

A common condition that affects twice as many women as men, irritable bowel syndrome (IBS) is often brought on by stress or anxiety and may follow severe intestinal infection. In some cases an intolerance to lactose (a sugar found only in milk) or high intakes of the sugar substitute sorbitol can trigger IBS. Symptoms, which many people put up with for years, include recurring and sometimes sharp abdominal pain, constipation and diarrhoea.

Avoiding stress and eating sensibly are the best treatments for IBS, though drugs may also be prescribed. Anyone with IBS should eat regular, moderate-sized meals. Aim for a high daily intake of soluble fibre from fruit such as apples, pears or dates, vegetables, and cereals such as oats, barley and rye. Avoid pulses: although they contain soluble fibre they also produce wind, which can make IBS symptoms worse. And stay away from bran, which irritates the intestine and aggravates the complaint.

Drinking plenty of water helps digestion and the elimination of waste products. And eating one or two portions a day of live yogurt will help to maintain a healthy balance of bacteria in the gut.

case study

Jane, 22, is a talented and successful cellist. For the past year she has had regular bouts of abdominal pain, abdominal bloating and intermittent diarrhoea, sometimes with nausea and headaches. Her GP confirmed her suspicion that she was suffering from IBS. She was advised to eat more soluble fibre and keep a food diary to identify any foods that precipitated symptoms (wheat is a common trigger). Having IBS diagnosed made Jane less anxious about her symptoms – which are now much reduced since she modified her diet and identified beans as her trigger food.

jams and spreads

However delicious they may be, jams and marmalades contribute very little to our diet nutritionally. Their main constituent is sugar, together with traces of fibre depending on the type of fruit used. Hardly any

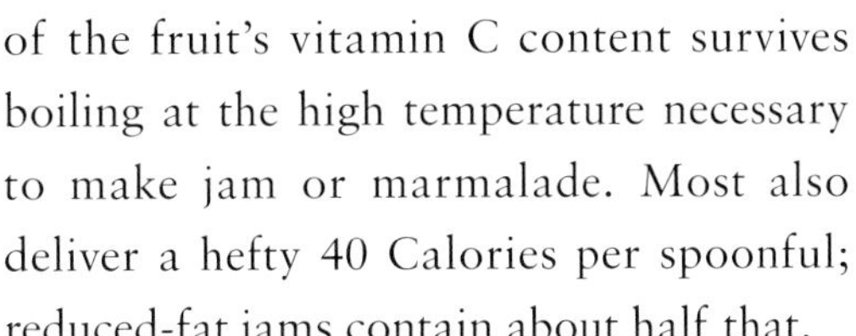

of the fruit's vitamin C content survives boiling at the high temperature necessary to make jam or marmalade. Most also deliver a hefty 40 Calories per spoonful; reduced-fat jams contain about half that.

Savoury spreads such as YEAST EXTRACTS tend to be high in sodium but are a source of B vitamins. Nut butters supply protein, but can cause allergic reactions. Peanut butter also contains significant amounts of niacin and potassium. Its fat content is mostly monounsaturates, which unlike saturated fat do not raise blood cholesterol.

benefit

Yeast extracts fortified with vitamin B_{12} are a useful source of the vitamin for vegans.

drawbacks

1 **Jams are particularly high in sugar.**

2 **Nut butters can cause an allergic reaction in susceptible people.**

jaundice

The two most common causes of jaundice are LIVER PROBLEMS and GALLSTONES, both of which can lead to a build-up of the bile pigment bilirubin in the blood. It is this pigment that gives the skin and eyeballs of jaundice sufferers their characteristic yellow tinge. Bilirubin is a by-product of the breakdown of red blood cells, and under normal circumstances is filtered out of the blood by the liver and excreted into the bile. If the liver is not working properly, this process is impaired. In all forms of jaundice the liver is struggling to cope, so avoid burdening it further. Cutting out alcohol and fatty foods will help, as metabolising both of these puts a heavy strain on the liver. Eating small, frequent meals and keeping to bland foods will give the liver a chance to recover.

Haemolytic jaundice is a specific type of illness caused by the excessive breakdown of red blood cells. In this case it may be helpful to eat foods that are rich in protein (such as fish), iron (such as lean meat) and B vitamins (such as pulses), in order to boost the production of replacement cells.

eat more

Eggs, dairy products, soya, fish and poultry if suffering from haemolytic jaundice.

eat less

Fatty and spicy food – strong spices tend to overstimulate the liver.

avoid

Alcohol.

kidney problems

drink more

Water – about 2 litres (3½ pints) a day.

eat more

Wholegrain cereals, for magnesium.

cut down on

1 Meat, fish and dairy produce.

2 Salt, sugar and alcohol.

Our kidneys maintain the body's delicate fluid balance by disposing of excess water, sodium, potassium and many waste products. They also activate vitamin D, make hormones needed for healthy bone marrow and red blood cell production, and control blood pressure. Poor kidney function increases the risk of infection and can lead to water retention, high blood pressure, ANAEMIA and kidney stones.

For healthy kidneys, drink about 2 litres (3½ pints) of fluid a day (preferably water) to 'flush' the kidneys and dilute substances for excretion. Limit your intake of animal protein (such as meat, fish, dairy produce), salt, sugar and alcohol as these can all put a strain on the kidneys.

Kidney stones are usually deposits of calcium and oxalate. Oxalate is made in the body and found in foods such as spinach and rhubarb. Some experts suggest that sufferers should limit their intake of these foods. Wholegrain cereals and other sources of magnesium may help to reduce stone formation. Cranberries may lower calcium levels in urine.

kiwi fruit

benefits

1 Excellent source of vitamin C.

2 Contain potassium.

3 Supply soluble fibre, which helps to lower blood cholesterol levels.

Only a few decades ago, these fruits were a rarity, known as Chinese gooseberries after their country of origin. Popularised in New Zealand and renamed after one of its national emblems, the flightless kiwi bird, they are now widely available.

The kiwi fruit is an excellent source of vitamin C. A single fruit provides the full adult daily requirement of the vitamin, which helps us to absorb iron from vegetables, and plays a vital role in wound healing and our immune system. Kiwi fruit also supply potassium, which helps to regulate the body's fluid levels and to ensure healthy blood pressure and a steady heartbeat. The soluble fibre in kiwi fruit can help to lower blood cholesterol levels: it binds to cholesterol and carries it out of the body as waste.

With around 10 per cent sugar, an average kiwi fruit provides about 30 Calories. Its flavour ranges from sweet to tart. (For the sweetest flavour, choose plump fruits that yield to gentle pressure.) Its bright green flesh does not discolour, making it a popular choice as an ingredient in fruit salad.

A kiwi fruit is an excellent
source of vitamin C and also
supplies soluble fibre.

Food labels tell us the facts, so we can choose between foods, compare value for money and eat healthily

labels

To protect us from any false claims and misleading descriptions, strict rules govern both the words and pictures used on food labels. By law, for example, a yogurt made with artificial raspberry flavouring but no real fruit cannot picture raspberries on the carton. And when a fruit yogurt claims 'now made with more fruit', the label or carton must state the percentage of fruit and provide the basis for comparison. A food label must state the product name, which must not be misleading – although exceptions are made for well-known foods such as cream crackers and Swiss rolls that are allowed to keep the names we all know them by because we're not likely to be misled. The label must list the ingredients, and give the weight or volume (an 'e' beside the figure indicates an average quantity).

By law, most foods – apart from non-packaged fresh meat, fish, fruit, vegetables – must also carry storage instructions and a datemark. Any packaged food beyond its 'use by' date could pose a health hazard, and must be removed from sale.

To make comparison between foods easy, nutrition information is always given per 100g or 100ml. Labels tell us how much energy, protein, carbohydrate, fat (saturates and non-saturates), sugars, fibre and sodium a food contains; they may also list vitamins and minerals.

Food labels must also carry the manufacturer's or seller's name and address. But if you are dissatisfied with a food product, first contact the shop where you bought it.

what's on the label?

1 The claim 'reduced calorie' means the food is lower in calories than the standard version: the total is given under 'Nutrition Information'.

2 Ingredients are listed in descending order of weight. This allows you to avoid products containing ingredients you don't wish to eat and makes comparing similar products easier.

3 Additives are listed by name or E number (or both) after a description of what they do. Flavourings must be mentioned, but not necessarily by name.

4 Genetically modified (GM) soya and maize must be identified as such.

5 Very perishable foods carry a 'use by' date. Others, such as frozen products, have a 'best before' date and safe storage instructions.

Less pungent than onions and just as versatile, leeks contain potassium and folate

leeks

A highly versatile vegetable, the leek is a member of the onion family and is similarly flavoured, though noticeably milder.

Leeks contain useful amounts of potassium, which is vital for maintaining the fluid balance in cells and tissues. It regulates blood pressure and heartbeat and is an important component in nerve function. Potassium also stimulates the kidneys into action and so leeks can act as a diuretic, helping to combat water retention.

Leeks also supply folate, needed for cell division and the formation of protein, DNA and RNA, and to guard against spina bifida in pregnancy. A 150g (5oz) portion of cooked leeks supplies nearly a third of the adult daily need and a sixth of the amount recommended during pregnancy.

Herbal remedies dating back to Roman times draw upon leeks to treat anything from kidney stones to sore throats. Their main drawback is their well-documented ability to cause wind – noted in Culpeper's *Complete Herbal* in the 17th century.

As with onions and garlic, handling leeks can cause contact dermatitis in sensitive people – wear rubber gloves while preparing them if you have delicate skin. After trimming and slicing leeks, rinse them well to remove soil trapped in their outer layers.

benefit

Contain useful amounts of potassium and folate.

drawbacks

1 **Can cause wind.**

2 **May cause contact dermatitis in susceptible people.**

lemons and limes

benefit

The juices are excellent sources of vitamin C.

drawbacks

1 Acidic juices, especially lemon juice, can erode tooth enamel.

2 Citrus fruit may be sprayed with fungicide and preservative.

Like all citrus fruits, lemons and limes are excellent sources of vitamin C. In the 18th century the British navy ordered ships to carry limes, to protect the crews against scurvy – a widespread disease caused by a severe vitamin C deficiency.

Today the fruits are used mainly in cooking, but mixing their juice with water to make a drink is a refreshing way to boost your vitamin C intake. Traditionally, a hot toddy – made with lemon juice, hot water and honey – is often prescribed for the early stages of a cold. The vitamin C in the juice helps the body fight infection and the honey eases a sore throat. Lime juice can be added to the drink instead of lemon.

Lime juice can also be used to tenderise meat and 'cure' raw fish. Dishes flavoured with lime rarely need salt – a helpful tip for anyone with high blood pressure who needs to cut down on salt.

Always scrub lemons thoroughly under running warm water if you are using the peel in cooking, as all but organically grown fruits are likely to have been treated with fungicide and preservative wax.

lettuce and salad

benefits

1 Very low in calories – unless smothered with mayonnaise or oil-rich dressing.

2 Contain folate and beta carotene, which the body converts into vitamin A.

3 Watercress and raw spinach are useful sources of iron.

You can eat as much lettuce and salad leaves as you like: they are 90 per cent water and contain very few calories – these only mount up if you add oily dressings.

Salad leaves of any kind supply folate and beta carotene (the vegetable form of vitamin A, vital for a healthy immune function). The darker green the leaves are, the more beta carotene they are likely to contain. But even if you eat a whole bowlful of salad at a sitting, your nutrient intake is unlikely to be significant, apart from useful amounts of phytochemicals. Spinach is an exception, but it is easier to eat a portion of cooked spinach than to munch through the same weight of raw spinach, and boiling does not affect its high beta carotene content. Watercress is also highly nutritious: 100g (3½oz) supplies 2.2mg of iron, a quarter of the recommended daily intake for a man – but that is a lot of watercress for one person to eat.

Lettuce has lately been joined by a host of continental cousins: look out for nutty lamb's lettuce, peppery rocket and slightly bitter radicchio (a red type of chicory).

Lemons, like limes, are excellent sources of vitamin C. A drink made with lemon or lime juice, hot water and a spoonful of honey is a traditional remedy for colds.

liver problems

eat more

1 Vitamin C-rich foods, such as oranges and kiwi fruit.

2 Vitamin B_{12}, found in liver, fish and dairy products.

3 Folate, found in liver, green vegetables and fruit.

cut down on

1 Saturated fats, sugar and alcohol.

2 Tea and coffee.

One of the largest of the body's organs, the liver performs many vital functions. As the body's chief detoxifier, it removes alcohol, nicotine, drugs and poisons from the bloodstream. It also makes bile, which is stored in the gall bladder then used to help digest fat. It regulates the body's blood sugar levels and stores surplus glucose as glycogen; it makes protein and breaks down any excess amino acids into urea for excretion; and it also stores vitamins A, B_{12}, D, E and K. Although it has a remarkable capacity for self-renewal, the liver can be damaged by disease brought on by viral hepatitis or by alcohol, which in severe cases causes cirrhosis. JAUNDICE, the result of a build-up of yellow bile pigment in the blood, is often a sign of liver failure.

To look after your liver, limit your intake of saturated fats, sugar, alcohol, tea, coffee and highly spiced foods. People with liver disease should boost their intake of B complex vitamins, including folate, to replace supplies depleted in the course of the disease; eat plenty of vitamin C-rich foods to promote recovery; and avoid all alcohol.

lupus

eat more

1 Fruit and vegetables.

2 Oil-rich fish such as sardines or salmon for omega-3 fatty acids.

3 Fortified breakfast cereals for vitamin D.

drink more

Water – at least 1.7 litres (3 pints) a day.

cut down on

Salt.

This disease, in which the antibodies of the immune system turn on the body's own tissues, has no known cause or cure. Lupus affects more women than men, and may start with headaches, tiredness and aching muscles or joints. Typical symptoms are a skin rash on the cheeks and over the nose, arthritis and progressive kidney damage. However, over time other organs of the body may also be affected.

Drugs help sufferers to manage the condition, but diet can also play a role. Fruit and vegetables should be eaten liberally unless the condition is severe, when the kidneys could be affected. Anyone with lupus should drink plenty of water to flush the kidneys, cut down on salt (which raises blood pressure) and avoid obesity.

Antioxidant vitamins and zinc, found in meat and dairy produce, help the immune system to function properly, and studies show that the fats in oil-rich fish can help ease inflammation. Since most people with lupus are sensitive to sunlight, they need to get their vitamin D from food sources such as eggs, milk and fortified cereals.

macrobiotic diet

The macrobiotic diet was developed in the early 1900s by an American-Japanese writer, George Oshawa. He believed that the diet, based on wholegrain cereals and vegetables, boosted energy and resistance to illness, so life could be lived to the full.

Macrobiotics is based on the Chinese philosophy of two opposing but complementary forces of nature: yin and yang. Yin is female; yang is masculine. People are predominantly yin (calm, creative) or yang (alert, energetic), but their physical and mental wellbeing depends on a healthy balance between the two. Foods, too, are said to contain yin and yang qualities. Yin foods include sugar, milk, tea, coffee, alcohol and most herbs and spices; yang foods include meat, poultry, fish, eggs, hard cheeses and salt. Central to the macrobiotic diet are foods with a harmonious yin/yang balance: wholegrain cereals, fresh vegetables, pulses, fresh fruit, nuts and seeds. There are seven levels of macrobiotic diet. Most are vegetarian, but some contain fish. The most extreme level consists of brown rice only and should not be tried.

benefits

1 Low in saturated fats and high in fibre.

2 May help reduce the risk of obesity, high blood pressure, cancer and raised cholesterol.

drawbacks

1 Unsuitable for children and pregnant women.

2 The brown-rice-only diet lacks adequate protein, iron, vitamin B_{12} and vitamin D.

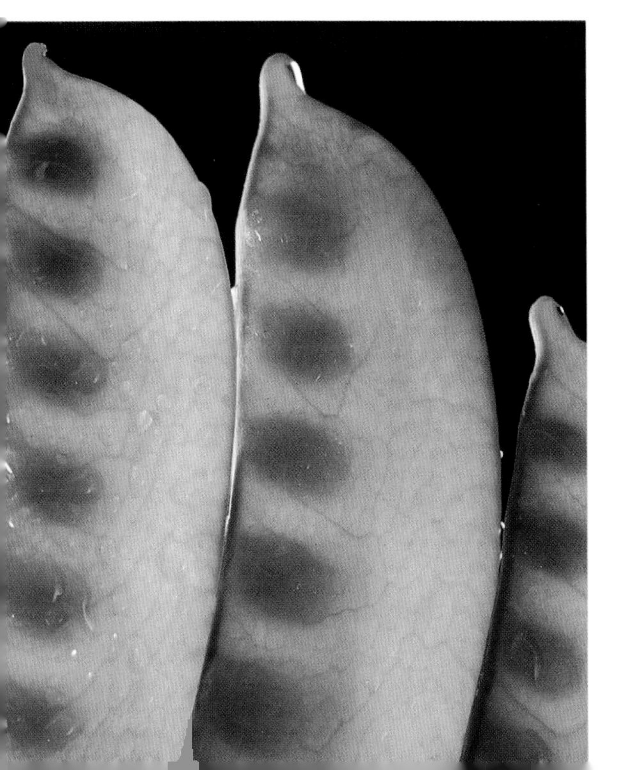

mangetout

As their French name – which means 'eat everything' – implies, these peas are eaten pod and all. They are an excellent source of vitamin C: a 100g (3½oz) portion served raw in a salad or lightly stir-fried provides 130 per cent of the adult daily requirement. Mangetout also contain beta carotene, the plant form of vitamin A; potassium, which helps regulate blood pressure; and some calcium and magnesium for strong bones and teeth and a healthy nervous system. The tiny peas in their bright green flat pods are also a useful source of fibre.

benefits

1 Excellent source of vitamin C.

2 Contain beta carotene, which the body converts to vitamin A.

3 Source of potassium, calcium and magnesium.

4 Supply useful amounts of fibre.

mangoes

benefits

1 Excellent source of beta carotene, which the body converts into vitamin A.

2 One medium-size mango supplies more than the adult daily vitamin C requirement.

A relative newcomer to the shopping aisles in Britain, the mango originated in India but is now grown throughout the tropics. A ripe fruit, which should yield to slight pressure, has smooth, orange-yellow flesh and is honey-sweet. It is rich in vitamin C and beta carotene, and in ANTIOXIDANTS which may help protect against certain cancers and heart disease. It is also high in sugar.

Eating a ripe, juicy mango can be a messy business. Try cutting a vertical slice either side of the stone and scoring each half into cubes, then slice the cubes off the skin.

meat and offal

eat more

1 Lean cuts – roast leg of lamb or rump steak.

2 Wild game – a low-fat source of protein, B vitamins and iron.

cut down on

1 Sausages, spare ribs and streaky bacon – they can be high in saturated fats.

2 Liver, kidney or heart if you are on a low-cholesterol diet.

Meat has always been prized for its high protein content, but it is also a source of many vital nutrients, including zinc, several B vitamins and iron in a form that is easy to absorb. Yet red meat fell from favour during the past decade because of consumer concerns about health risks linked to it. So how good is meat for you?

Beef

Beef supplies most of the nutrients we need to stay healthy, so it is not surprising that Britain was once a country of committed beef eaters. A succession of health scares changed all that. Chief among these was BSE (bovine spongiform encephalopathy) or Mad Cow Disease. When official scientists finally conceded that the cattle disease may also infect humans – in the form of Creutzfeldt-Jakob Disease – the government imposed new regulations for the beef industry and drastically restricted meat sales. Most beef is now deemed safe to eat, but for the moment beef on the bone and some types of offal are still banned.

Another source of controversy has been farmers' use of growth hormones in cattle.

Since no one knows what impact these drugs may have on humans, they have been prohibited by the EU. Consumer fears about fat content have also undermined beef's popularity. In response, farmers are now breeding leaner cows. Lean beef contains less than 5 per cent fat, under half of which is saturated. As a result, beef is now less likely to raise cholesterol levels and increase the risk of heart disease.

Lamb

Lamb has a reputation for being the fattiest of meats. However, modern breeding techniques favour leaner animals and lamb in fact contains little more fat than beef or pork. The fat content depends on the cut. Leg is the leanest, shoulder one of the fattiest. Since saturated fats raise cholesterol, fatty cuts are best eaten in small quantities.

Lamb is high in protein and most vitamins and contains zinc and iron. The colour of the meat varies with the season and is a clue to quality. Good spring lamb should be dark pink with white fat. Winter lamb is a darker red, with a creamy fat.

Pork

Pork is often assumed to be a high-fat food, and therefore associated with increased risk of heart problems. In fact, pork is one of the leanest meats, not much fattier than skinless chicken. It probably owes its bad reputation to pork pies, spare ribs, streaky bacon and cheap sausages, which are high in saturated fats.

Pork is a good source of B vitamins, especially thiamin (B_1), which is vital to the body's energy supplies. It also contains zinc and iron. The healthiest way to prepare it is to trim off excess fat then roast or grill it. Cook it thoroughly, to destroy the parasites that pork sometimes harbours.

Our ancestors used to cure pork – salting or smoking it to produce ham – to preserve it.

Lamb is an excellent source of protein. It also contains most vitamins, as well as the minerals zinc and iron.

avoid

1 **Undercooked beefburgers. They could be infected with the bacteria *E. coli*, a source of food poisoning.**

2 **Overcooked beefburgers from a barbecue. Some scientists claim charred meat may contain carcinogenic (cancer-causing) chemicals.**

3 **Liver, if you are pregnant. It is very high in vitamin A, which in excessive quantities can cause birth defects.**

This process survives to this day, largely because we enjoy the flavour. However, people who suffer from high blood pressure should limit their intake of these sodium-rich products.

Game

Any wild animal that is hunted for food is known as game. In Britain that includes pheasant, partridge, grouse, rabbit, hare and venison. Many nutritionists consider wild game to be healthier than farmed meat because there generally tends to be less fat on a bird or animal that has lived an active life in a wild habitat.

Like other meats, game is a good source of protein, B vitamins and iron. It is rich in potassium, which helps to regulate the body's fluid balance and maintain a steady heartbeat. It also contains phosphorus for healthy bones and teeth.

Offal

The term offal is applied to any edible part of an animal, except the flesh. It includes liver, kidneys, brain, stomach (tripe), heart, tail, tongue and feet. Offal is generally rich in B vitamins, iron and zinc. However, liver, heart and kidney can be high in cholesterol and so are not recommended for anyone following a low-cholesterol diet.

Liver is an exceptionally good source of easy-to-absorb iron and is often prescribed for those suffering from iron-deficiency ANAEMIA. It also supplies vitamin B_{12} (vital for red blood cell formation and the nervous system), and vitamin A (essential for healthy skin and for the immune system).

After the BSE crisis, the government banned the sale of certain types of offal in any food products. These include brain, spinal chord, thymus gland (sweetbreads), spleen and intestines.

how much fat?

meat	total fat(g)	saturated fat(g)
BEEF		
Roast sirloin	21.1	9.0
lean meat only	9.1	3.7
Grilled rump steak	12.1	5.2
lean meat only	6.0	2.5
Stewed mince	15.2	6.5
LAMB		
Roast leg	17.9	8.9
lean meat only	8.1	3.9
Roast shoulder	26.3	13.1
lean meat only	11.2	5.4
Grilled loin chops	29.0	14.4
lean meat only	12.3	5.9
PORK		
Roast leg	19.8	7.3
lean meat only	6.9	2.4
Grilled loin chops	24.2	9.0
lean meat only	10.7	3.8

All figures per 100g (3½oz)

Some medicines, especially those taken over a long period, may influence what we should eat

medicines

Most medicines have no effect on our nutritional needs, but nutrients and drugs do not always interact harmoniously. Sometimes one can prevent the other from doing its job efficiently. Even some non-prescription drugs can upset the balance of nutrients in the body. Antacids, taken mainly for indigestion, can limit absorption of phosphorus, a mineral essential for healthy bones. Laxatives, which speed up the workings of the bowel, can deplete the body of water and certain nutrients, such as potassium. For these reasons, antacids and laxatives should be used sparingly.

Aspirin, the non-prescription pain reliever, can sometimes depress levels of folate, which is very important during pregnancy. Antibiotics can have negative effects, too. As well as destroying the 'bad' bacteria that cause infections, they can wipe out the 'friendly' bacteria that help to maintain the health of the digestive system. To restore a healthy balance, you should eat live YOGURT. (Note, however, that calcium-rich foods can impair the actions of certain antibiotics. Check first with your doctor, and if necessary eat yogurt only after you have completed the course of medication.)

Jim, who is 55, has high blood pressure but controls it with an antihypertensive drug that is called a calcium antagonist. When his GP first prescribed the drug, Jim was advised to forgo his morning glass of grapefruit juice as it would increase the concentration of the drug in his bloodstream. His doctor explained that grapefruit juice has this effect on a variety of drugs. Missing his morning grapefruit juice, Jim tried an antihypertensive drug that was compatible with the juice. But it proved less effective at controlling his blood pressure. He now starts the day with orange juice – and peace of mind.

eat more

1 **Fibre-rich foods, such as bran, to reduce reliance on laxatives.**

2 **Live yogurt, if you have been on antibiotics. It helps to restore the bacterial balance in the gut and to prevent thrush.**

3 **Foods rich in potassium, such as bananas, and calcium, such as milk, if you are on diuretics, to offset losses of these minerals.**

4 **Folate-rich vegetables and pulses if you take aspirin regularly or are on non-steroidal drugs.**

cut down on

1 **Saturated fat if you are on steroids or to help cholesterol-lowering drugs do their job more effectively.**

2 **Fibrous foods if you are taking digoxin for your heart. They reduce absorption of the drug.**

avoid

1 Alcohol: it intensifies the toxic side effects of most drugs and undermines the effectiveness of several.

2 The antimalarial drug pyrimethamine if you are pregnant. It may reduce absorption of folate, which could increase the risk of birth defects.

Pills prescribed to promote heart health can deplete our nutrient levels. Certain cholesterol-lowering medicines, for example, reduce absorption of iron and folate. On the other hand, too much vitamin A or C, chiefly in supplement form, can sabotage the work of anticoagulants (used to prevent blood clotting). If you are taking such drugs, ask your doctor if dietary changes are necessary.

Diuretics, which increase urine output and are prescribed for fluid retention, can flush vital nutrients from the body; calcium and potassium are the two most common casualties. Some nutritionists recommend supplements to make good the loss. Most other nutrients can be replaced with a healthy diet. Steroids (anti-inflammatory drugs) call for a diet low in saturated fat as they can raise cholesterol levels. The non-steroidal drug sulphasalazine, prescribed for rheumatoid arthritis, and cytoxic drugs, used in chemotherapy, can reduce folate levels. Diet can help restore the loss, but avoid supplements: too much folate can reduce effectiveness of the medication.

melons

benefits

1 Melons are a low-calorie source of potassium, which helps balance sodium intake.

2 Cantaloupe melon is rich in both vitamin C and beta carotene.

The best-known varieties of melon are cantaloupe, watermelon and honeydew. All are high in water and low in calories: depending on the type, a 100g (3½oz) serving contains up to 31 Calories. Melons also contain potassium and vitamin C. Cantaloupe, the orange-fleshed variety, is the most nutritious. A 100g (3½oz) portion supplies more than half the daily vitamin C requirement and plenty of beta carotene, which the body converts to vitamin A. These ANTIOXIDANT vitamins may help to protect against cancer and heart disease.

menopause

The menopause is a term that describes the transitional phase in a woman's life when she stops menstruating. The process usually starts in the mid-forties or fifties, when levels of the hormones progesterone and oestrogen drop. Symptoms can include hot flushes, insomnia, hair loss, mood swings and fatigue. Bone mass also declines, increasing the risk of OSTEOPOROSIS, and there is a greater chance of heart disease.

Many women decide to take Hormone Replacement Therapy (HRT) to reduce the risk of these diseases, and to relieve menopausal symptoms. However, diet may also help. Eating more calcium can help keep bones strong, while a low-fat diet helps to maintain a healthy heart and to prevent the unwanted weight gain often associated with menopause.

Some experts argue that certain foods can do the job of HRT. Recent research has focused on plant substances called phytoestrogens, which partially imitate human oestrogen and are abundant in soya beans. Many women claim that vitamin E, found in avocados and nuts, alleviates hot flushes.

eat more

1 **Soya products. Their phytoestrogens may help relieve symptoms.**

2 **Dairy products, to supply calcium for strong, healthy bones.**

cut down on

1 **Tea and coffee: they speed calcium excretion, and aggravate insomnia.**

2 **Salt, which can cause fluid retention, a problem experienced by menopausal women.**

menstrual problems

While some women sail through their monthly period, others can suffer a whole host of discomforts. These can begin anywhere from mid-cycle onwards and go on until the end of menstruation. They include cramps, backache, fluid retention, anxiety, fatigue, depression, headaches, food cravings and breast tenderness. They are known collectively as premenstrual syndrome (PMS), and may be related to changing hormone levels.

Dietary strategies can sometimes help to relieve PMS symptoms. Generally, women who eat a well-balanced diet – low in fat and high in carbohydrate – appear to suffer less with PMS. Foods rich in vitamin B_6 (such as meat and whole grains) are thought to be particularly helpful, as they may reduce fluid retention and cramping pain as well as depression.

Women afflicted with especially painful periods (a condition known as dysmenorrhoea) should try to increase their intake of vitamins C and E, and calcium and magnesium. Vitamin C is in most fruits and vegetables; vitamin E is in wheatgerm and

eat more

1 **Meat and green leafy vegetables for vitamin B_6, which may relieve painful spasms.**

2 **Vitamin E-rich foods, which may help reduce breast tenderness.**

3 **Potassium-rich foods such as bananas, which help reduce fluid retention.**

4 **Iron-rich foods such as red meat, if you have heavy bleeding.**

cut down on

1 Salt, which can cause water retention, a symptom of PMS.

2 Alcohol, which aggravates mood swings, another feature of PMS.

3 Tea, coffee and cola-based drinks, as some studies suggest caffeine aggravates PMS.

eggs; calcium is in dairy products; and magnesium is in shellfish and nuts. These nutrients may aid relaxation and relieve muscular spasms and cramping sensations.

Some PMS sufferers crave sweet foods and tend to feast on sugary snacks. A sugar 'high', however, can lead to an energy crash, triggering headaches and fatigue. So it is preferable to eat small meals regularly, to keep blood sugar levels balanced. Other women crave salt, but this is best eaten sparingly, too: it can encourage fluid retention and make the whole body feel puffy.

Women who suffer from heavy periods (menorrhagia) may also benefit from dietary changes. When women lose more blood than usual, they can succumb to ANAEMIA. In this case, it is essential to eat plenty of iron-rich foods, such as meat and green leafy vegetables. Unusually heavy blood loss should be investigated by your doctor. Other conditions that call for medical attention include: frequently missed periods (amenorrhoea, which may be caused by dramatic weight loss), irregular bleeding, and severe abdominal pain.

metabolic problems

food note

Babies suffering from PKU have difficulty processing breast or cow's milk and are often fed on special formula instead. They should also avoid any food containing the artificial sweetener aspartame.

Every chemical reaction that occurs in the body is triggered by a catalyst known as an enzyme. A deficiency or defect in one of these enzymes can cause various diseases, known collectively as metabolic disorders. These rare conditions tend to be inherited, and symptoms usually show up at, or soon after, birth. Early diagnosis is essential to prevent physical or mental abnormalities developing. A few metabolic disorders can be treated with diet, including the best known, phenylketonuria (PKU), for which every newborn is tested routinely. It results from an inability to metabolise an amino acid, phenylalanine, found in protein-rich foods. Treatment involves cutting down on these foods. Other inherited disorders include: Refsum's Disease, which is caused by defective enzymes needed to metabolise phytanic acid in fish and dairy products; Maple-syrup Urine Disease, characterised by an inability to process amino acids, which are excreted in sweet-smelling urine; galactosaemia, triggered by a failure to metabolise milk sugar (lactose) and galactose. All are treated with exclusion diets.

Choose your carton of milk wisely and you can reap significant nutritional benefits

milk and cream

Packed with vitamins and minerals, milk has long been considered nature's perfect food. Although full-fat milk is high in saturated fat, which is now associated with heart problems, there are lots of low-fat varieties to choose from. Virtually fat-free milk supplies almost all the nutrients of full-fat milk, with a fraction of the fat.

Milk's prime nutritional asset is its calcium content, crucial for healthy bones: 568ml (1 pint) supplies the total recommended daily intake for adults. Calcium derived from other food sources, such as vegetables, is less readily absorbed. Milk also provides protein, zinc, phosphorus, B vitamins and vitamin A. However, when the fat content is reduced by skimming, fat-soluble vitamin A is lost. Dried milk retains all its nutrients except for some losses of vitamins B_1 and B_{12}.

For most of us, the slimmed-down varieties of milk are the healthiest. Virtually fat-free milk contains just 0.1 per cent fat; half-fat 1.6 per cent; full fat around 4 per cent. A 500ml (18fl oz) carton of virtually fat-free milk has around 165 Calories, half that of full-fat milk. However, low-fat milk is not suitable for children under five: their growing bodies need the energy from fat.

Most milk sold in England and Wales and all milk sold in Scotland is pasteurised, or heated to destroy any harmful bacteria. (UHT milk is heated to an even higher temperature, to extend its shelf life.) After it has been pasteurised, milk may be homogenised, to stop the cream rising to the top. Pasteurised milk should last for between three and five days in the fridge.

Some people have problems digesting cow's milk as their body does not produce enough lactase, the enzyme that breaks down lactose (milk sugar). The symptoms can include bloating, diarrhoea, stomach cramps and skin rashes. Treatment involves finding alternatives to cow's milk, such as rice, almond or soya milk. (See ALLERGIES.)

Cream, still considered a treat by many, is not popular among the health conscious. While it contains valuable amounts of vitamin A, as well as calcium and phosphorus, it is also high in saturated fat. Single cream contains 18 per cent fat; double cream 48 per cent and whipping cream 40 per cent. So try to keep cream for special occasions.

benefits

1 Milk is a rich source of easily absorbed calcium, for strong bones and teeth, and contains a range of other minerals and vitamins.

2 Virtually fat-free or half-fat milk contains as much calcium as full-fat milk.

drawbacks

1 Cream is high in saturated fat and calories. Clotted cream has some 586 Calories per 100ml (4fl oz).

2 Unpasteurised milk can cause food poisoning.

food note

For anyone on a low-fat diet, fromage frais, with only 0.2-7 per cent fat, is a good substitute for cream.

Minerals are the building blocks of life. Our daily diet must deliver a range of them to guarantee good health

minerals

eat more

1 Green leafy vegetables and sardines (with their bones). These are good sources of calcium and iron.

2 Vitamin C-rich foods, such as oranges. They enhance the absorption of iron from vegetables.

3 Potassium-rich foods such as bananas. They can help offset the ill-effects of excessive sodium intake, such as high blood pressure.

4 Wholegrain cereals. They supply chromium and magnesium.

5 Brazil nuts. They contain selenium, an antioxidant mineral.

6 Shellfish and sunflower seeds. They are excellent sources of zinc.

Like vitamins, minerals are nutrients that we cannot live without. They perform vital processes in the body – from fortifying teeth and bones to maintaining a healthy immune system. In recent years, scientists have investigated possible links between them and major diseases, including osteoporosis, diabetes, heart disease and cancer.

Minerals are the basic elements of the earth's crust. They are absorbed by plants, which are then eaten by animals and humans. The amount we get from our food often depends on levels in the soil where our food originated. Calcium, zinc and iron are among the minerals we are most likely to be short of. However, a balanced diet should supply all those we need.

In the body, minerals are stored mainly in bone and muscle tissue, but their influence is all-pervasive. More than 60 have been identified, and several (including those discussed below) are said to be 'essential'. By this, scientists mean the minerals carry out at least one activity upon which life, growth or reproduction depends.

Vitamins and minerals interact with each other. Often one cannot operate without another. Vitamin D, for example, is needed for calcium absorption; vitamin C will enhance iron uptake. Sometimes one will undermine another. For example, too much phosphorus can inhibit the effectiveness of calcium and magnesium.

Calcium

Calcium is crucial to strong bones and teeth – indeed 99 per cent of it is stored in them. Growing awareness of the brittle-bone disease OSTEOPOROSIS, which mainly affects post-menopausal women, has made this mineral the focus of much public interest lately. Studies now suggest that an adequate intake, from infancy onwards, can help prevent this condition.

Aside from building and strengthening our bones, calcium has other vital jobs. It is necessary for blood clotting, muscle contraction (which includes regulating heartbeat) and nerve transmission. It also participates in certain digestive processes.

Calcium cannot function by itself. To absorb the mineral, we need vitamin D. Calcium deficiency often results from a lack of vitamin D, which is produced when the skin is exposed to sunlight. Hence lack

of sunlight can lead to children getting rickets, a softening of the bone causing bow legs. Conversely, certain substances sabotage the effectiveness of calcium. Caffeine, wheatbran and salt, for example, either inhibit absorption or speed excretion. Oxalic acid, found in rhubarb and spinach, can also reduce absorption.

Magnesium

This is another mineral that promotes strong teeth and bones. It also helps the body absorb and use other minerals and vitamins, including calcium and vitamin C. There is now substantial scientific evidence to confirm that magnesium also assists in regulating heartbeat.

Magnesium is essential for the smooth operation of muscles and nerves. One of its vital functions is to help muscles contract. This explains why deficiencies are often associated with muscle spasms and convulsions. A shortage can also lead to anxiety, extreme apathy and high blood pressure.

Phosphorus

Like calcium, phosphorus helps build bones and teeth, where most of it (80 per cent) is found. However, too much can be counterproductive. An excess of this mineral can reduce calcium absorption, raising the risk of OSTEOPOROSIS. It will also hinder the absorption of magnesium.

It is vital to maintain a healthy balance of calcium and phosphorus. This is not difficult to do, since most foods that supply calcium give us phosphorus, too. The equilibrium is disrupted only if you overindulge in refined foods, fats and fizzy drinks. All of these tend to be short on calcium and long on phosphorus.

Phosphorus is also vital for the release of energy in cells, and for the absorption and transport of nutrients.

Potassium

Those who reach for the salt-cellar every meal will need plenty of potassium. This is because sodium and potassium perform a

Cheese is rich in calcium; wholegrain cereals supply magnesium; and oysters are an excellent source of zinc.

food note

Minerals are classified in three groups:

1 Macrominerals are needed in the largest quantities and include calcium and potassium.

2 Microminerals are needed in smaller amounts and include iron and zinc.

3 Trace elements are required in minute proportions and include selenium and iodine.

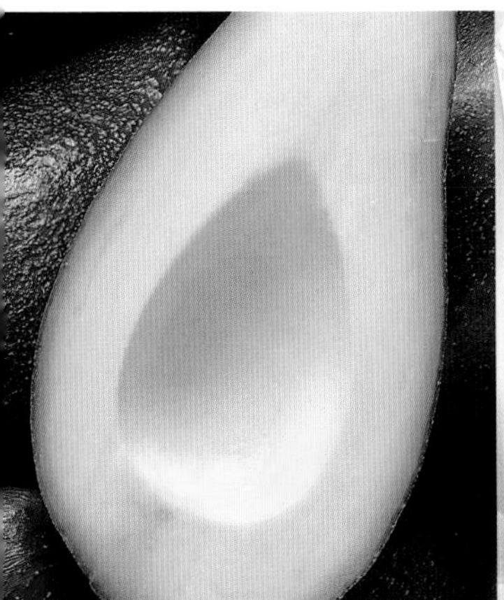

Avocados are a good source of potassium; milk is rich in calcium; sardines supply iron.

cut down on

1 Spinach and rhubarb with your major source of calcium. They contain oxalic acid, which can prevent absorption of the mineral.

2 Alcohol. It can inhibit absorption of zinc.

balancing act in our bodies. (See also SALT AND SODIUM.) They work together to regulate fluid balance, heart rhythm, and nerve and muscle functions. When potassium levels rise, sodium levels dip, and vice versa. So potassium-rich foods help offset the effects of excessive sodium intake – namely fluid retention and high blood pressure.

Some medications, such as diuretics and drugs to control blood pressure, may prompt potassium loss. Symptoms are listlessness, confusion, thirst and an abnormal heartbeat. For most of us, a balanced diet will supply the potassium we need. Levels are regulated by hormones and any excess usually acts as a diuretic. However, anyone with kidney problems should avoid high intakes: they cannot expel it efficiently and may experience heart problems.

Chromium

Chromium is essential for maintaining healthy blood sugar levels. It boosts the effectiveness of insulin, which regulates glucose levels in our blood. Sufficient chromium is essential for diabetics. A chromium deficiency can also lead to high blood cholesterol levels, since this mineral helps to control proportions of fat and CHOLESTEROL in the blood.

Iron

Lethargy and breathlessness are among the first signs of an iron deficiency. That is because this mineral is vital to the body's oxygen supply. It is essential for production of haemoglobin, the pigment in red blood cells that transports oxygen around the body. It is also needed for the making of myoglobin, a similar pigment that stores oxygen in muscle.

Iron has many other functions, too. It is present in various enzymes, sparking essential chemical changes. For instance, it helps stimulate the conversion of beta carotene (found in highly coloured foods, such as carrots) into vitamin A. This is vital for good night vision and a healthy immune system, among other things. Iron also plays a role in keeping your teeth, bones and immune system in good shape.

So how much iron do you need? That depends on who you are. Menstruating women need more than men, and anyone with an ulcer, or something that raises the risk of bleeding, should ensure that they are getting enough. Pregnant women need plenty to sustain their growing child. The baby will draw all it wants from the mother, but that could leave her short.

There are two types of iron in food: haem iron, derived from meat; and non-haem iron, from plants and grains. Only 10 per cent of non-haem iron is absorbed, compared with 25 per cent of the meat-derived variety. However, we can boost absorption of plant-derived iron by combining it with foods rich in vitamin C, such as oranges.

Selenium

Most recent interest in selenium has centred on its cancer-protective potential. It is an antioxidant mineral. In other words, it helps limit cell damage caused by free radicals – unstable molecules associated with cancer and other degenerative diseases.

It is also essential for normal growth and fertility, proper functioning of the liver, and hormone production. We need it to keep hair and skin healthy, and to preserve our eyesight, too. The amount of selenium in food depends on local soil conditions.

Zinc

Zinc is critical for reproduction and for growth. A shortage in childhood can slow development. It is also key to a healthy immune system, so is vital for anyone susceptible to infections, such as the elderly.

This mineral helps keep our senses sharp, too. It is necessary for night vision and our ability to taste and smell. Indeed, a jaded appetite is one of the first signs of a zinc deficiency. Among other red flags are slow wound healing, and a low libido. The latter could explain the reputation of oysters – a zinc-rich food – as an aphrodisiac. However, don't expect zinc to raise sex drive above its natural level.

avoid

1 **Excessive intakes of caffeine, which can inhibit effective use of both calcium and iron.**

2 **Too many fizzy drinks, which can upset the balance of calcium and phosphorus.**

3 **Long-term use of antacids, which can deplete phosphorus.**

4 **Too much potassium if you suffer from kidney disease. If the kidneys can't expel the mineral efficiently, it could trigger heart problems.**

Nuts are a useful source of several minerals, including phosphorus, iron and copper.

minerals

mineral	good sources	what it does	daily needs	symptoms of deficiency
macrominerals (needed in large amounts)				
CALCIUM	Milk, cheese, yogurt, canned sardines (with bones) and green leafy vegetables.	Vital to build bones and teeth; helps regulate heartbeat and other muscle contractions; and is necessary for normal blood clotting.	700mg	Soft and brittle bones, fractures and osteoporosis. Muscle cramps and weakness.
CHLORIDE	Table salt (sodium chloride) and foods that contain it.	Maintains the body's fluid balance. An essential component of the gastric juices in the stomach.	2,500mg	A normal diet will always supply sufficient chloride.
MAGNESIUM	Leafy green vegetables, wholegrain cereals, wheatgerm, pulses and nuts.	Essential component of bones and teeth; helps ensure smooth functioning of nerve and muscles, including regulating heart rhythm.	Men: 300mg Women: 270mg	Lethargy, fatigue, cramps and muscle tremors, heart-rhythm abnormalities.
PHOSPHORUS	Fish, meat, poultry, dairy products, eggs, beans and nuts.	Vital for energy production; helps to build and maintain healthy bones and teeth; facilitates absorption of many nutrients.	550mg	In rare instances, prolonged use of antacids may cause a deficiency. Excessive intake can reduce absorption of calcium and magnesium.
POTASSIUM	Oranges, bananas, avocados, nuts and seeds, potatoes, pulses, dried fruit and milk.	Together with sodium, helps to regulate the fluid balance within cells and maintain normal blood pressure. Vital for muscle contraction and nerve impulses.	3,500mg	Weakness, confusion and severe thirst. In extreme cases, a deficiency could trigger abnomal heartbeat and serious respiratory problems.
SODIUM	Table salt (sodium chloride), smoked and cured foods, many processed foods.	Together with potassium, regulates the body's fluid balance; essential for nerve and muscle function.	1,600mg	Deficiency is highly unusual, but can lead to low blood pressure, dehydration and muscle cramps. Excess causes water retention and high blood pressure.

mineral	good sources	what it does	daily needs	symptoms of deficiency
microminerals (needed in small amounts)				
CHROMIUM	Red meat and liver, egg yolks, cheese, seafood and wholegrain cereals.	Needed for the regulation of blood sugar levels; also helps to keep blood cholesterol levels in check.	25mcg	May impair the action of insulin and the regulation of glucose in the blood.
COPPER	Offal, oysters and some other types of shellfish, nuts and seeds, mushrooms and cocoa.	Needed to build bones and cartilage and other connective tissue. Helps the body absorb iron from food. Helps protect against excess free radicals, which may lead to cancer.	1.2mg	Deficiency found only in premature babies or in infants with malabsorption conditions.
FLUORIDE	Tea, toothpaste and tap water.	Helps to prevent tooth decay.	No set dietary requirement	Tooth decay. Excess causes weak, discoloured teeth and brittle bones.
IODINE	Seafood, iodised table salt and seaweed.	Needed for the thyroid gland to function normally.	140mcg	Goitre (enlargement of the thyroid), lethargy, coarse skin and hair.
IRON	Lean meat, offal, sardines, egg yolks, fortified breakfast cereals and green leafy vegetables.	Needed to help the body convert food into energy and to make haemoglobin, which carries oxygen in the blood.	Men: 8.7mg Women: 14.5mg	Breathlessness, fatigue, anaemia, lowered resistance to infection.
MANGANESE	Pulses, cereals, brown rice, wholegrain bread and nuts.	Plays an essential role in allowing the body to produce energy. Helps to build bones and connective tissue.	1.4mg	No symptoms.
MOLYBDENUM	Offal (especially liver), whole grains, yeast, pulses, and green leafy vegetables.	Needed to make DNA (which contains all our genetic information); it also helps to fight tooth decay.	50-400mcg	Deficiency is unknown.
SELENIUM	Meat, fish, citrus fruit, dairy products, Brazil nuts, avocados and lentils.	Antioxidant mineral that protects against damage caused by excess free radicals, which can lead to cancer and heart disease. Also essential for normal sexual development.	Men: 75mcg Women: 60mcg	Rare, but could hamper growth, retard sexual development and reduce fertility. Excess causes hair loss and fatigue.
SULPHUR	Protein from animal and vegetable foods.	Found in every cell in the body, it is a component of two essential amino acids that help to form many proteins.	No set dietary requirement	Deficiency is unknown.
ZINC	Oysters, red meat, sunflower seeds and peanuts.	Needed for normal growth, sexual development and reproduction, and a healthy immune system.	Men: 9.5mg Women: 7mg	Reduced immunity. In adolescents, impaired development.

Many everyday foods can have a significant effect on the way we feel and even how we behave

mood and diet

eat more

1 Bananas, oats, wholemeal bread, dried fruits, potatoes (all complex carbohydrates) for a gentle lifting and calming of the spirits.

2 Fruit, for vitamin C and sweetness without the drawbacks of refined sugary foods.

3 Foods rich in vitamin B (brown rice, fortified breakfast cereals, liver, yeast extract, walnuts, watercress and sesame seeds).

4 Lean red meat, sardines, eggs and dried apricots, for iron.

5 Shellfish, pumpkin seeds, nuts, liver (unless you are pregnant) and lean meat, for zinc.

The connections between food and mood are complex: blood sugar levels, adverse reactions to food and nutritional deficiencies can all influence our mental state.

Mood swings often stem from low or fluctuating BLOOD SUGAR LEVELS resulting from irregular eating patterns. If you eat a sugary snack on an empty stomach, the effects can be felt in minutes. The rapid rise in blood sugar stimulates the pancreas to secrete extra insulin to convert it into fuel; then the sugar level drops again quickly. This can lead to renewed hunger and, in extreme cases, causes dizziness, headaches, tearfulness, irritability or aggression. To prevent this effect, keep sugar levels stable by having small meals often and combining sweet foods with fibre and complex carbohydrates to slow down sugar absorption: a bowl of oat cereal, fruit crumble or dried fruits, for example. This strategy can help women who suffer from pre-menstrual mood swings and sweet cravings.

Although alcohol is renowned for inducing relaxed, sociable moods, these effects are short-lived. Alcohol is in fact not a stimulant but a depressant and, if taken on an empty stomach, its impact is the same

case study

Peter, a 33-year-old teacher, visited his GP, concerned about sudden changes in mood. He found that eating chocolate helped to lift his spirits and he was irritable if he missed his daily fix. The GP advised Peter to cut out chocolate, refined sugars, tea, coffee and alcohol, all of which can contribute to mood swings. He suggested eating more foods high in tryptophan – fish, chicken, cottage cheese, avocados and wheatgerm – which help to stabilise moods. He also recommended regular exercise. Within a few weeks, Peter found he was much more mellow – even with his most difficult class.

as that of sweet foods: blood sugar levels soar but then drop again, prompting a 'blue' mood. Excessive consumption can lead to changes in personality, and aggression. Caffeine is another potent mood influencer. Its initial effect may be greater alertness, but it can become addictive and cause jitteriness and irritable behaviour.

As chocolate contains caffeine, it can boost alertness, and the 'feel-good' factor it delivers is partly due to a chemical in cocoa called phenylethylamine that occurs naturally in the brain and has an uplifting effect. Yet the instant blood sugar fix from chocolate tends to be followed by a low when sugar levels fall again.

Children are particularly vulnerable to the mood swings that chocolate and sweets bring; see-sawing blood sugar levels may contribute to tantrums and restlessness. Links between food and HYPERACTIVITY are still contentious but changes to diet have resulted in marked improvements in some children. This condition seems to be exacerbated by certain foods, which cause an allergic reaction or contain compounds that the child cannot metabolise because of an enzyme deficiency. Avoiding certain ADDITIVES – notably tartrazine (E102) and benzoic acid – found in orange squash, sweets, soft drinks and processed products, may help to lessen symptoms, while some children improve after avoiding salicylates (in most fruits and in aspirin).

Food alone cannot cure clinical depression, but a nutritious diet can lift people out of a low period. Sometimes sadness or negativity are due to imbalances in brain chemicals known as endorphins. In these cases, carbohydrate foods can help because they boost production of the endorphin known as serotonin, which promotes calm and happy feelings. Bananas, sweetened milk drinks and high-fibre sweet foods such as wholemeal scones will lift moods without incurring the slump that follows a snack made mainly from refined sugar.

Depression often brings a loss of appetite, just when a wholesome diet is most needed. Sufferers may develop nutritional deficiencies, especially of B vitamins, vitamin C, iron and zinc; and malnourishment contributes to moods sinking even lower. Whole grains, pulses, lean meat, nuts and eggs all supply B vitamins and valuable minerals, while fruit and vegetables provide vitamin C. High doses of vitamin B_6 (found in yeast extract, wheatgerm, liver, bananas, eggs and soya beans) have proved effective in relieving pre-menstrual depression.

cut down on

1 **Sweets, chocolate and refined biscuits and cakes.**

2 **Sugary drinks.**

3 **Alcohol.**

4 **Caffeine in coffee, tea and cola drinks.**

5 **Processed foods and drinks high in additives.**

mushrooms

benefits

1 Good source of copper, for iron absorption and healthy bone growth.

2 Contain potassium and phosphorus.

drawback

Some wild mushrooms are highly poisonous.

There are more than 2,500 varieties of mushroom grown worldwide, with the more unusual varieties that are increasingly available – cep, chanterelle, morel and oyster – tasting distinctly different from the familiar button or field mushrooms.

Mushrooms are a good source of copper, which helps the body absorb iron from food; they contain potassium, which helps to regulate blood pressure, and phosphorus, for healthy teeth and bones. Raw mushrooms also contain small amounts of folate, needed for red blood cell formation, and other B vitamins. Many practitioners of traditional Chinese medicine have long prescribed oriental varieties of mushroom – shiitake, rieshi, maitake, for instance – for immune-system diseases and even cancer. However, these medicinal properties have yet to be confirmed by clinical studies.

Depending on where they grow, mushrooms can accumulate toxic metals such as cadmium or lead. You should never pick wild mushrooms unless you are certain you can identify them. Many are poisonous but look very similar to edible varieties.

nail problems

eat more

1 Liver (unless you are pregnant), lean meat, oil-rich fish and leafy vegetables, for iron.

2 Shellfish, fish, lean meat, wholegrain cereals and nuts, for zinc and selenium.

3 Brown rice and fortified breakfast cereals for B vitamins.

avoid

Tea at meals: it inhibits iron absorption.

Our nails are made of a protein called keratin, which is also the main component of our hair and outer layer of our skin. Healthy fingernails tend to grow slightly faster than toenails – about a millimetre a week (more in hot climates). The condition of our nails is a good indicator of our general state of health, and also signifies any nutritional deficiencies.

Pale, thin, spoon-shaped nails, especially on the thumb, may indicate iron deficiency or anaemia, or a lack of zinc. Zinc deficiency can also cause small white flecks in nails and brittle nails that split. Wide ridges may indicate selenium deficiency. Narrow ridges and fragile nails may signal a lack of B vitamins. Contrary to popular belief, calcium does not strengthen nails.

Whitlows are an infection of the nail bed caused by a bacterium that enters the skin where it is broken, often due to a hangnail. They are common among diabetics and people whose hands are often immersed in water. Treatment is with anti-fungal ointments, but a balanced intake of vitamins and minerals also helps healing.

Packed with nutrients, nuts are also high in calories

nuts

All types of nuts – almonds and hazelnuts in particular – are rich in the antioxidant vitamin E, which helps to protect against heart disease. They also provide B vitamins, needed to produce energy in cells. However both vitamin E and the B vitamin thiamin are destroyed by roasting.

Nuts supply protein and minerals, including iron, potassium, calcium, magnesium, phosphorus and copper. Almonds are a useful source of calcium for vegans: 100g (3½oz) provides a third of the adult daily requirement. However, the protein in nuts is incomplete: it lacks adequate amounts of the range of amino acids the body needs to make its own protein. A vegan diet that provides all the essential amino acids will include bread, grains and pulses.

Because they are high in fat, nuts are full of calories. Most contain more than 600 Calories per 100g (3½oz), though chestnuts have only 170. Walnuts are especially rich in the essential omega-6 and omega-3 fatty acids (see FATS), which help reduce the risk of heart disease. Two recent US studies suggest that walnuts and almonds can help to reduce blood cholesterol levels.

what's in nuts?

ALMONDS
An excellent source of vitamin E, manganese and phosphorus; a rich source of copper and magnesium; a good source of riboflavin; and a useful source of calcium, zinc and iron*.

BRAZIL NUTS
An excellent source of vitamin E, copper and phosphorus; a rich source of manganese; a good source of selenium and zinc; and a useful source of iron* and riboflavin.

CASHEWS
An excellent source of copper and manganese; a rich source of phosphorus, magnesium and zinc; a good source of iron* and zinc; and a useful source of vitamin B_6, vitamin E and folate.

HAZELNUTS
An excellent source of vitamin E and copper; a good source of magnesium and phosphorus; and a useful source of vitamin B_6, folate, iron*, manganese, riboflavin and zinc.

PEANUTS
An excellent source of manganese and niacin*; a good source of copper, magnesium and phosphorus; and a useful source of vitamin B_6, vitamin E and zinc.

WALNUTS
An excellent source of vitamin E, iron and manganese: a good source of magnesium and phosphorus; and a useful source of folate.

*Daily requirements for men and women vary

benefits

1 Excellent source of vitamin E.

2 Supply B vitamins, minerals and protein for vegetarians.

3 Walnuts and almonds may help reduce the risk of heart disease.

4 Almonds are a useful source of calcium, for vegans.

safety first

1 Nuts may trigger an allergy in some people: in rare cases peanut allergy can be fatal.

2 Young children risk choking on nuts.

3 Unless stored in a cool, dry place, nuts may develop potentially harmful moulds.

oils

benefits

1 Provide essential fatty acids.

2 Good source of vitamin E.

3 Essential for the absorption of fat-soluble vitamins A, D, E and K.

drawback

Excessive consumption can lead to weight gain.

Whereas animal FATS are high in saturated fats, most oils are rich in monounsaturated and polyunsaturated fats. These can help to lower blood cholesterol levels, particularly if you limit the saturated fats in your diet. Vegetable oils also provide essential fatty acids (omega-6 and omega-3 families), which the body cannot manufacture. These are needed for growth; they also encourage healthy blood circulation and reduce inflammation. Omega-6 fatty acids are abundant in sunflower and safflower oil, while the omega-3 group (found in oil-rich fish such as mackerel, salmon and sardines) is available from vegetable oils such as soya bean and oil seed rape.

Oils are rich in vitamin E, an antioxidant that helps to protect against cancer. Like all fats, oils aid absorption of fat-soluble vitamins A, D, E and K. However, as oils are calorie-rich (30g/1oz has 225 Calories), they can cause weight gain if consumed to excess. Coconut and palm oils are high in saturated fats, so use them sparingly. Never re-use oil for frying; repeated heating causes carcinogenic substances to form.

old age

eat more

1 Lean meat and fish.

2 Whole grains, fruit and vegetables for nutrients and fibre.

3 Low-fat dairy products for calcium.

cut down on

High-fat foods such as cakes, biscuits and crisps; bacon, sausages and salamis; full-fat dairy products.

As we age, we tend to become less active and more prone to weight gain. Energy requirements fall as our bodies lose muscle tissue and our metabolism becomes less efficient, but we need a high intake of vitamins and minerals to compensate for less efficient absorption and use.

A healthy diet for an elderly person should include plenty of foods that are highly nutritious but low in fat, such as lean meat, fish, cereals, fruit and vegetables. Elderly people's diets are often low in vitamin B_{12} and folate. Meat is a good source of vitamin B_{12}, while folate is found in green, leafy vegetables, wheatgerm, pulses and fortified breakfast cereals.

Post-menopausal women need a high calcium intake, from low-fat milk and dairy products, to guard against OSTEOPOROSIS, or brittle bones. Extra vitamin D, from oil-rich fish, eggs or supplements, may also be needed by house-bound people whose skin is rarely, if ever, exposed to sunlight.

Elderly people should try to take regular exercise to maintain a healthy weight and prevent disorders associated with obesity.

Olive oil and soya oil
can help to lower blood cholesterol levels.

onions

benefits

1 Help to lower blood cholesterol levels and reduce the risk of heart disease.

2 Help to prevent blood clotting.

drawbacks

1 Raw onions make your breath smell.

2 Can cause wind.

3 May trigger migraine in susceptible people.

If research backs up some of the current thinking on onions' health-giving properties, they could eventually be valued as a medicinal superfood and not simply as the tasty base for countless savoury dishes. Scientists are not yet able to endorse many of the claims, but it does appear that eating raw onions may help to reduce blood cholesterol levels. This is thought to be because they increase levels of high-density lipoproteins (HDLs) that shift cholesterol away from the artery walls and hence reduce the risk of 'furred-up' arteries. It also seems that both raw and cooked onions may contain a substance that helps stop blood from clotting and even stimulates the breakdown of existing clots. This is good news for anyone who suffers from poor circulation or heart disease.

The sulphur compounds that give onions their smell are also under investigation to see if they can inhibit cancer-cell growth.

oranges

benefits

1 Excellent source of vitamin C.

2 Also contain pectin, which is thought to help lower blood cholesterol.

drawback

A common trigger of migraine in susceptible people.

An average orange contains more than the recommended daily amount of vitamin C needed to keep an adult in good health. As vitamin C helps our bodies fight off infection and is essential for healthy teeth, bones, gums and skin, perhaps 'An orange a day keeps the doctor away' would be a more appropriate adage than the traditional reference to an apple a day.

Vitamin C improves iron absorption from plant foods, making orange juice an ideal mealtime drink. But although the juice is high in vitamin C, potassium and folate, it is no substitute for the whole fruit. The membranes around each segment contain pectin, a form of soluble fibre that is thought to help lower blood cholesterol levels. Bioflavonoids are also found in the membranes: their antioxidant properties, combined with those of vitamin C, help guard against damage to cells by free radicals, which can lead to cancer.

Non-organically grown oranges are likely to have been sprayed with fungicide and preservative, so scrub them thoroughly in warm water before you grate the peel.

Foods grown without chemicals may be kinder to the environment but are they really better for our health?

organic foods

Cereals, fruit and vegetables can only be sold as organic if they are grown without fertilisers or pesticides on soil that has been free from these chemicals for at least two years. Organic meat must come from free-range livestock fed mainly on organic food and not treated routinely with antibiotics or other drugs. In Britain, organic farms are certified and regularly inspected by those organisations that belong to the UK Register of Organic Food Standards (UKROFS), the government body that is responsible for enforcing EC law. The Soil Association is considered to have the highest standards of all the various approved organic-symbol organisations.

Growing fears over food safety and damage to the environment have increased the consumer demand for organic produce. There have been a number of reports of high levels of pesticides in foods, such as organo-phosphates in fruit and vegetables and lindane in cow's milk, highlighting the pitfalls of intensive farming. More than 25,000 tonnes of pesticides are used in Britain every year. Despite this, however, the latest government survey showed that less than 1 per cent of the foods tested had residue levels above the legal maximum limit, and approximately two-thirds had no detectable residues at all.

The claim that organic produce is nutritionally superior to non-organic has yet to be scientifically proven, but many people seem to prefer its taste. To keep up with the growing demand, new organic foods are launched almost weekly – including pastas, sauces, baked beans, biscuits, chocolate, ice cream and baby foods.

Organic fruit and vegetables are usually more expensive to buy and often look inferior to those produced by conventional farming methods. Because they are not chemically treated, they may also spoil more quickly. Currently, less than 1 per cent of all the food produced in Britain is organic, so most organic produce on our supermarket shelves is imported. However, the government's Organic Aid Scheme, recently introduced to provide financial support for those farmers wishing to convert to organic farming, may increase the availability of British-grown organic food in the coming years.

benefits

1 **Produced without chemical fertilisers and pesticides, which some people think may be harmful to health.**

2 **Many people believe that organic foods taste better.**

3 **Food is produced by environmentally friendly farming practices.**

4 **Organic famers tend to have higher standards of animal welfare.**

drawbacks

1 **Some organic foods tend to be more expensive than foods that are produced by conventional farming methods.**

2 **Organic fruit and vegetables can spoil more quickly.**

osteoporosis

eat more

1 Calcium-rich foods such as dairy products.

2 Oil-rich fish and eggs for vitamin D.

avoid

1 Alcohol and smoking.

2 Excessive intakes of foods rich in phytic and oxalic acids, such as wheat bran, nuts and rhubarb.

A common condition among the elderly, osteoporosis leads to a loss of bone density, making bones fragile and susceptible to fractures. It occurs more frequently in women, particularly after the menopause when decreasing levels of the hormone oestrogen accelerate the weakening of bones. Recent research suggests that eating calcium-rich foods and taking regular exercise during childhood and adolescence is the most effective way of preventing osteoporosis. However, a deficient diet can speed up bone loss in people who already have the condition. To increase your intake of calcium and vitamin D, which play major roles in bone formation, include plenty of dairy products, bread and oil-rich fish in your diet. Clinical trials have shown that calcium and vitamin D supplements slow down bone loss and reduce fractures.

Avoid consuming excessive amounts of wheat bran, pulses, nuts and seeds, which are high in phytic acid, and of rhubarb and spinach, which contain oxalic acid. Both of these substances can significantly reduce the uptake of calcium in the body.

papayas

benefits

1 Excellent source of beta carotene, which the body converts to vitamin A.

2 Rich in vitamin C.

Orange-fleshed papayas are an excellent source of beta carotene, the plant form of vitamin A, which is essential for growth and normal cell division. In addition, a whole fruit supplies more than twice an adult's daily requirement of vitamin C. Both beta carotene and vitamin C act as antioxidants, neutralising the free radicals that can damage cells and increase the risk of cancer. Papayas also provide dietary fibre, potassium (which helps to counteract the effects of excessive sodium intake) and some calcium (for strong teeth and bones).

parsnips

In common with other root vegetables such as beetroot and carrots, parsnips have a high natural sugar content, providing the equivalent of a teaspoonful of sugar per 100g (3½oz) portion. They also contain starch (about half the amount that is present in potatoes) and are a good source of dietary fibre, which helps to maintain a healthy digestive system.

Parsnips are a useful source of potassium, needed to maintain normal blood pressure, and they also provide some calcium and magnesium. Unlike carrots, they contain hardly any beta carotene (the plant form of vitamin A). However, they do provide useful amounts of vitamin C (a medium-sized serving supplies a quarter of an adult's daily requirement) and vitamin E. They are also a useful source of folate, which is essential for red blood cell formation.

Parsnips vary in colour from pale yellow to creamy white. They are at their most tender when about the size of a large carrot; larger parsnips may be tough and woody. To preserve their sweet flavour, cook them until they are just tender.

benefits

1 Good source of starch and dietary fibre.

2 Contain vitamin C, folate and potassium.

pasta

Once considered stodgy and fattening, pasta has now taken its rightful place as an important part of a balanced diet. Made from water and durum wheat semolina (a coarse, high-protein flour), it is available fresh and dried in many shapes. Egg is sometimes added to enhance the flavour; and spinach, beetroot, tomato purée and saffron can be used to alter the colour.

Pasta is easy to cook and low in fat: only if you add rich ingredients such as butter, cream and cheese do the calories in a pasta dish soar. It is a good source of complex carbohydrates, providing both resistant starch, which is broken down slowly in the body to boost energy reserves, and fibre, which helps maintain a healthy digestive tract. Pasta also provides B vitamins such as thiamin and riboflavin, particularly if it is made from wholewheat flour.

In the Far East, noodles form the base of a variety of low-fat dishes. They can be made from wheat, but also potato, rice or mung bean flour, which can be useful alternatives for people with COELIAC DISEASE who need a gluten-free diet.

benefits

1 Good source of complex carbohydrates.

2 Low in fat.

drawback

Wheat-based pastas are unsuitable for people with coeliac disease.

peaches and nectarines

benefits

1 **Rich sources of vitamin C.**

2 **Dried peaches are a good source of iron and potassium, but are high in calories.**

A sweet, juicy peach is surprisingly low in calories. A single 100g (3½oz) ripe fruit contains only 30 Calories yet provides over three-quarters of an adult's daily vitamin C requirement. Its soft flesh is easy to digest and has gentle laxative properties.

Canning peaches in sugary syrup, however, robs them of about 80 per cent of their vitamin C, and adds lots of calories.

Dried peaches make a healthy, nutritious snack as they provide useful amounts of iron, potassium and beta carotene, the plant form of vitamin A. They also offer a concentrated source of energy. Weight for weight, dried peaches contain six times the calories of fresh peaches.

The word nectarine derives from the Greek *nektar*, meaning the drink of the gods in Greek mythology. Originally cultivated from peaches, nectarines are sweeter and more nutritious: one fresh, average-sized nectarine supplies 40 Calories and nearly all an adult's daily requirement of vitamin C. Unlike peaches, nectarines do not continue to ripen once picked, so only buy fruits that are already soft.

pears

benefits

1 **Good source of soluble fibre.**

2 **Rarely, if ever, provoke intolerance or allergic reactions.**

There are hundreds of varieties of pear, but the best known are Conference, Comice, Gold Williams and Red Williams.

An average-sized pear contains about 70 Calories, mostly in the form of natural fruit sugars that the body can process quickly and easily into energy. Pears are also useful fibre providers: a typical unpeeled pear contains 3.4g. Like apples, they are a good source of pectin, the soluble fibre that has been found to protect against cancer of the colon and also help to lower levels of cholesterol in the blood. Although their vitamin C content is not significant, pears supply flavonoids, which function as antioxidants. In addition, the fruit contains small amounts of boron, a trace mineral that is believed to stimulate electrical activity in the brain and thus improve mental alertness.

As pears are among the few foods that very rarely cause allergies or other adverse reactions, they are especially valuable for weaning babies and for anyone following an exclusion diet (used to help identify sources of food allergies).

One average-sized peach contains only 30 Calories and yet – unpeeled – provides more than three-quarters of an adult's daily requirement of vitamin C.

peas

benefits

1 Fresh peas are a good source of thiamin.

2 Both fresh and frozen peas contain useful amounts of vitamin C.

If you grow your own peas, you will know that the quicker you get them from garden to table, the better they taste. As soon as the pods are picked, the sugars in peas begin to convert into starch, and they start to lose their sweet flavour. Freezing arrests this process, and commercial growers can freeze their crop almost as soon as it is picked, preserving not only the sugar but also the vitamin C levels. Peas contain more vitamin C than other fresh legumes. Fresh peas are a good source of thiamin, which our bodies need to release energy from food as it is broken down. A 50g (2oz) serving of boiled fresh peas provides nearly half the adult recommended daily amount; a similar portion of boiled frozen peas provides about a sixth. Peas also contain some fibre, folate and phosphorus.

peppers and chillies

benefit

Sweet or bell peppers are an excellent source of vitamin C.

drawbacks

1 The skin of green peppers tends to be waxy, making them difficult to digest.

2 Chilli peppers can irritate skin and mucous membranes.

Sweet or bell peppers are an excellent source of vitamin C (vital for healthy teeth, gums, bones and skin), and also contain useful amounts of beta carotene, the plant form of vitamin A (essential for good eyesight, healthy skin and an efficient immune system). The colour – whether it's green, red, orange or yellow – depends on the variety and the stage of ripeness. Red peppers contain the highest levels of beta carotene. Chopped peppers are refreshing in summer salads, while serving them chargrilled barely affects their nutrient content.

Chilli peppers are more often used as a spice than a vegetable, as their fiery heat severely restricts how many you can eat. Mild chillies do exist, though, and chilli specialists have a whole vocabulary to describe their heat rating. The compound that is responsible for chillies' fire power is capsaicin. This is most concentrated in the seeds and pith, which is why recipes advise removing the seeds before adding chillies to a dish. Wash your hands thoroughly after preparing them: no one who rubs their eyes after chopping chillies ever forgets it.

pickled foods and chutneys

Pickling prevents the growth of microbes that normally cause foods to decompose, and has been used for centuries to preserve fruit and vegetables. Pickles are generally made by adding hot or cold vinegar to the raw foods, or by cooking them in vinegar; this destroys most vitamins, but minerals usually survive. A third pickling method, by which cucumbers or gherkins, for example, are treated with salt to lower their moisture content before being bottled in vinegar, eliminates minerals as well as vitamins and greatly increases salt levels.

Although sauerkraut is often described as 'pickled cabbage', it is actually a fermented food that is surprisingly rich in vitamin C: a 100g (3½ oz) serving provides around a quarter of the adult daily requirement.

Pickles, chutneys and relishes are usually eaten in small dollops, which is the best policy. Chutneys, especially fruit chutneys, can be high in sugar, and pickles are best avoided by those on low-salt diets. Pickles and chutneys may trigger allergic reactions as some contain tyramine, histamines or salicylates, which are all known allergens.

benefit

Sauerkraut is a useful source of vitamin C.

drawbacks

1 High in salt.

2 May cause allergic reactions.

safety first

Never reduce the sugar or salt in pickle or chutney recipes, as the botulism bacteria may survive and cause severe food poisoning.

piles

Haemorrhoids (to use their medical term) are varicose veins in the anus. Symptoms include itching, soreness, bleeding, and pain when coughing, laughing or sitting on the toilet. Piles are often hereditary, but they can also be brought on by chronic CONSTIPATION, obesity or pregnancy.

As constipation and straining to pass a bowel motion are often the outcome of a diet that contains a lot of refined foods and not enough fluids, mild cases of piles can be treated by drinking at least 2 litres (3½ pints) of water daily and eating more high-fibre foods. The soluble fibre in oats, pulses and most fruit and vegetables is especially effective for constipation and piles because it eases bowel motions by forming soft, moist stools.

Piles can be extremely painful and should never be trivialised: the earlier they are treated, the better. Ointments, suppositories or injections may be prescribed, or even – in severe cases – surgery.

Never ignore bleeding: this can indicate a serious disorder such as liver disease or rectal cancer, so consult your doctor.

eat more

Apples, pears, prunes, oats and pulses for soluble fibre.

drink more

Water and other fluids.

cut down on

1 Refined foods.

2 Hot, spicy foods such as curries, and Mexican and chilli dishes, which aggravate the condition.

pineapples

benefits

1 Aid digestion.

2 May prevent blood clotting.

3 May relieve arthritis and speed recovery from injuries.

Scientists have recently claimed that pineapples may have some interesting and useful medical benefits. A 100g (3½oz) portion of raw pineapple contains 41 Calories, plus potassium and some vitamin C, but it is an enzyme called bromelain that is the particular focus of attention.

Bromelain appears to aid digestion by breaking down protein, and is also thought to inhibit blood clots and 'furring' of the arteries, making it especially beneficial for sufferers of heart disease and strokes. In addition, bromelain has achieved dramatic results as an anti-inflammatory agent in the treatment of arthritis, as well as in speeding up the process of tissue repair after sprains, sports injuries and surgery.

To derive any of these benefits, eat fresh pineapples: although canning leaves vitamin C intact, it destroys the bromelain. (Note that in rare instances fresh pineapple can cause an allergic reaction.)

Gargling with pineapple juice is a traditional folk remedy for sore throats, while the fruit itself is sometimes prescribed for catarrh, bronchitis and indigestion.

plums and prunes

benefits

1 Plums are low in calories.

2 Prunes are effective natural laxatives.

3 Prunes may help ward off certain cancers.

Ripe, juicy plums provide some vitamin E, an antioxidant that may help to protect against certain cancers and to slow some of the effects of aging, such as wrinkling. However, the vitamin E is lost when plums are dried to form prunes.

Like all dried fruits, prunes are a concentrated source of energy, yet they contain fewer calories than other types: 100g (3½oz) provides 161 Calories compared with 250 Calories from the same weight of sultanas. They also supply useful amounts of potassium, iron and vitamin B_6. Prunes are renowned for their laxative properties. This is largely because of their high levels of the soluble fibre pectin, which is also effective in reducing blood cholesterol, and because they contain isatin, a substance that stimulates the bowel muscles. Prune juice is a good alternative for those who dislike eating whole prunes.

Recent studies show that prunes may help in the fight against cancer: when tested for their ability to absorb damaging free radicals (unstable molecules that can cause cancer), they outperformed all other fruit.

potatoes

The British derive more vitamin C from potatoes than from any other food, and they are not as fattening as many people think. A medium-sized potato is high in carbohydrates and also contains protein, fibre and potassium. (It is the butter or oil they are often cooked in that adds the fat.)

sweet potatoes

The wholesome sweet potato comes in two varieties: the moist, orange-fleshed type (often mistakenly referred to as a yam) and the dry, creamy-fleshed kind. Both contain potassium, vitamin C and fibre, but the orange-fleshed potato is also an excellent source of beta carotene, one of the antioxidants that can protect against cancer and the ill-effects of aging.

Their natural sweetness intensifies during storage and cooking. Because of their rich flavour, they are often assumed to be high in calories. In fact, a 100g (3½oz) serving contains 84 Calories, not much more than an ordinary white potato.

Eating potatoes in their skins is preferable: they are high in fibre and nutrients are found just beneath the skin. The vitamin C levels fall once potatoes are lifted, so freshly harvested ones are the best source. Vitamin C is also lost in cooking: mashed potato has the least, and baked the most.

The much-maligned chip is actually highly nutritious if prepared the right way. The healthiest kind are thickly cut – rather than thin or crinkle-cut – because they have a smaller surface area, relative to their weight, to absorb fat. Cooking them in polyunsaturated vegetable oils or olive oil (as opposed to peanut or palm oils or animal fats), and blotting them on absorbent paper, will further reduce fat content. Crisps are undoubtedly high in calories, but they are rich in potassium and vitamin C, and many healthier low-salt, low-fat versions are now available.

benefits

1 Valuable source of carbohydrate, potassium and vitamin C.

2 Low in calories if cooked healthily.

drawback

Chips, crisps and roast potatoes can be high in fat.

food notes

1 Green and sprouted potatoes contain solanine and chaconine, which are toxic, so any with green patches should be discarded.

2 Diabetics should be aware that, compared with resistant starches, potato starch causes a rapid rise in blood sugar levels.

Even before a woman conceives, her diet can have an effect on the development and health of her baby

pregnancy

During its time in the womb, a baby is completely dependent on its mother's body for the nutrients it needs to grow and develop. For this reason, a pregnant woman who eats a well-balanced, varied diet increases the likelihood of having a healthy baby. Although pregnant women are often said to be 'eating for two', this is certainly not necessary, in terms of calorie intake at least. No extra calories are needed for the first six months of pregnancy, and only around 200 extra Calories per day are required for the last three months. In general, a healthy diet – high in complex carbohydrates and fresh fruit and vegetables, and low in saturated fats, salt and sugar – should provide all the nutrients that both mother and baby require.

Diet during the three to six months prior to conception and during the first 12 weeks of pregnancy, when the embryo develops all its major organs, is particularly important. Avoid alcohol completely or reduce intake to a minimum (no more than one unit per day) before the woman begins to try to conceive, and maintain it at this level throughout pregnancy. Consuming more than 15 units of alcohol a week poses a serious threat to the baby's development. From conception until the 12th week of pregnancy, expectant mothers should take a daily supplement of 400mcg of folic acid, as this significantly reduces the risk of the baby suffering from spina bifida. Dark green leafy vegetables, nuts and pulses are useful dietary sources of folic acid.

A number of minerals and vitamins are especially important during pregnancy. Calcium is crucial for the formation of the baby's teeth and bones, so pregnant women should aim to eat two or three portions of calcium-rich food a day. Dairy products, canned sardines and green leafy vegetables all provide calcium. Its absorption is aided by vitamin D, found in oil-rich fish and margarine. Zinc, available from red meat, wholegrain cereals, nuts and sunflower seeds, is essential for the baby's general growth and the development of its immune system. Omega-3 fatty acids (found in oil-rich fish such as salmon and sardines) is crucial for the development of the baby's brain. Iron, which is used to make the baby's blood and is vital for the mother's health as well, is in high demand during pregnancy. Sources include lean meat, sardines and egg yolks. Combining iron-rich vegetables with vitamin C, from citrus fruit or juice, for example, helps to increase the amount of iron absorbed by the body.

A number of foods may present certain dangers to the unborn baby and these should be avoided throughout pregnancy. Some cheeses (soft, ripened varieties and blue-veined), unpasteurised dairy products and pâté are all possible sources of listeria, which can cause miscarriage or premature birth. Likewise cook-chill meals must be served piping hot to be completely safe. Raw or soft-boiled eggs (and anything containing them, such as homemade mousses, ice cream or mayonnaise), undercooked poultry, poor-quality shellfish, and smoked or cured meat may all contain salmonella so are also best avoided. Very high intakes of vitamin A from animal sources have been linked to birth defects, so liver and all liver products should not be eaten during pregnancy. Toxoplasmosis, which can cause blindness or brain damage, may be present in unpasteurised dairy products, raw or undercooked meat or soil clinging to fruit and vegetables. Pregnant women should wash their hands after handling raw meat, ensure all meat is well cooked, and wash all fresh vegetables thoroughly. (To protect the baby from toxoplasmosis, pregnant women should also avoid handling cat litter, and wear gloves while gardening.)

A healthy diet, high in complex carbohydrates, fresh fruit and vegetables, and low in saturated fats, should provide all the nutrients both mother and baby need.

Morning sickness (which can strike at any time of day) affects seven in ten pregnant women, although it usually passes after the first three months. Nausea can be relieved by eating little and often – fresh ginger may help to alleviate the problem. A deficiency of zinc may make women more susceptible. Constipation is a common problem during the middle and later months. Gradually increasing fibre intake, with foods such as wholemeal bread, bran breakfast cereals, baked beans and peas, and drinking plenty of water, may help to relieve it.

eat more

1 **Red meat for zinc, to aid the development of the baby's nervous and immune systems.**

2 **Dairy products for calcium, needed for healthy bones and teeth in mother and baby.**

3 **Sardines, eggs and fortified cereals, for the extra iron needed during pregnancy.**

cut down on

Alcohol – no more than one unit per day.

avoid

1 **Soft cheese, blue-veined cheese and pâté; and unpasteurised dairy products (all possible sources of listeria).**

2 **Raw or soft-boiled eggs, shellfish and undercooked poultry (all of which can contain salmonella).**

3 **Liver and liver products, which contain high levels of vitamin A.**

4 **Raw or undercooked meat and unwashed fruit and vegetables (all possible sources of toxoplasmosis).**

Follow a few simple rules before, during and after cooking and you can be sure of really nutritious meals

preparing and cooking food

health tips

1 Always thaw frozen food completely before cooking.

2 Never refreeze frozen food after it has been thawed.

3 Don't reheat food more than once. Repeated reheating destroys nutrients and encourages bacterial growth.

4 When reheating leftovers, make sure the food reaches 75°C (167°F) throughout.

5 Always cook food thoroughly, especially meat, fish and eggs.

6 As soon as food is cool, put it in the refrigerator.

Most meals that we eat at home involve some preparation and cooking as well as storing – even if it's just defrosting a frozen lasagne and putting it in the oven.

Always be scrupulous about HYGIENE when handling food. To minimise the risk of FOOD POISONING, keep raw and cooked foods in separate, covered dishes in the fridge, with raw meat and fish on the lowest shelf so they cannot drip on to any other food. Be sure to wash your hands, chopping boards and knives – between handling raw and cooked food – and clean the taps afterwards, too.

When cooking or reheating food, make sure it is cooked or heated all the way through before serving it. This is particularly important with microwave ovens, which can sometimes cook food unevenly. Never reheat leftovers more than once; and never defrost frozen food then refreeze it. You can thaw some raw mince, make a lasagne and freeze that, but never refreeze the uncooked mince.

Serve all hot foods piping hot, straight from the oven, and cold food, cold. Store all perishable foods in the fridge – both before they're cooked and once prepared if you are not going to eat them immediately. And, as flies spread bacteria, cover any foods laid out on a table before serving, particularly in summer.

Some nutrients – mainly vitamins – are lost when foods are cooked. To reduce vitamin loss, chop vegetables into large chunks just before you cook them; and cook them briefly in the minimum of water or in a microwave oven. Rapidly stir-frying vegetables in just a little oil helps to seal in water-soluble B vitamins and vitamin C.

Try to reduce – and maybe even eliminate – the salt you add when cooking, and instead use herbs or spices to flavour a dish. Soya sauce, a popular alternative to salt, is high in sodium, so use it sparingly.

To reduce the fat added during cooking, try to grill, bake, boil, steam, microwave – or even dry-fry – foods whenever possible. When you do cook with fat, choose olive, sunflower or rapeseed oils – all high in unsaturated fats – in preference to butter or lard. And rather than pouring oil into a frying pan, try using a hand spray filled with oil to give the pan a light coating.

processed foods

Canning, freezing, drying and smoking are all examples of commercial food processing, without which much of the world's food would be wasted. Although some nutrients are lost in processing, quality produce that has been quickly processed at source is often more nutritious than 'fresh' food that has been displayed for a few days.

The heat treatment used in canning kills bacteria, extends shelf-life, and makes protein and starches easier to digest. But there is also some loss of vitamins, namely thiamin (B_1), riboflavin (B_2) and vitamin C. Nutritionally, frozen food is often very close to fresh equivalents, but frozen vegetables and fruit lose some water-soluble vitamins when blanched before being frozen. The reason frozen food does not keep as long as canned food is that, even at subzero temperatures, certain vitamins and fats oxidise during prolonged storage.

Dried foods lose much of their vitamin C and some beta carotene (with freeze-drying less vitamin C is lost). Smoked foods tend to be high in sodium, and some meats, such as ham, contain nitrates and nitrites.

benefits

1 **Processed foods have longer storage life.**

2 **Processing reduces any risk of food poisoning.**

drawback

There is often some loss of nutrients, particularly vitamin C and other water-soluble vitamins, during processing.

protein

Proteins are essential constituents of every cell in the body. They are necessary for growth and development in children, for maintenance and repair of cells in adults, and for the production of enzymes, antibodies and hormones: in short, they are essential to keep the body working. Proteins are made up of building blocks called amino acids, of which there are some 22. The body can make most of these, but there are eight that it is unable to make, which are called essential amino acids. Protein is found in a variety of foods: meat, fish, dairy products, eggs and soya beans each contain all the essential amino acids and are therefore complete dietary sources. Beans and other pulses, nuts, seeds and cereals are good sources of protein but do not contain adequate amounts of the full range of essential amino acids, so vegetarians need to eat a variety of them to get all the nutrients they need. Nutritionists advise that 10–15 per cent of our daily energy intake should come from protein. Very high protein diets are best avoided: they can strain the liver and the kidneys.

food note

The average daily intake of protein in the UK is 85g for men and 62g for women. A protein intake above 1.5g per kilogram of body weight is not recommended. A woman of 60kg (9½ stone), for example, should not have more than 90g.

Beans and lentils supply protein, fibre and energy

pulses

benefits

1 Good source of protein.

2 Provide soluble fibre, which can help lower blood cholesterol.

3 Rich in complex carbohydrates for a steady stream of energy.

4 Soya beans contain phytoestrogens that may help to protect against certain cancers.

drawbacks

1 May cause flatulence.

2 Kidney beans need correct cooking to eliminate toxins.

3 Soya beans may cause an allergic reaction in susceptible people.

Beans, peas and lentils, collectively known as pulses, are the dried seeds of the legume family. As an alternative to meat, they are a good source of protein. When combined with rice, bread and other cereal products, they can form part of a vegetarian or vegan diet that delivers all the amino acids essential for growth and development.

Pulses are rich in complex carbohydrates. The starch they contain is a good source of energy and is converted to glucose slowly in the body, making pulses valuable for diabetics, who need to control blood sugar levels. Pulses provide soluble fibre, which may help to lower raised blood cholesterol levels, and insoluble fibre, which helps to prevent constipation. They also provide useful amounts of B vitamins and minerals such as iron, calcium and potassium.

All canned pulses come ready to eat. Uncooked varieties, with the exception of lentils and split peas, should be soaked in water for eight to 12 hours then boiled for 15 minutes, drained and simmered in water until soft. Soaking helps to eliminate the indigestible sugars that cause wind.

In the case of kidney beans, soaking is essential to prevent food poisoning. Raw kidney beans contain a substance that cannot be digested in the stomach without a thorough soaking first.

Soya beans are rich in phytoestrogens, hormone-like chemicals that may help to protect against cancers of the breast, bowel and prostate, and the brittle-bone disease osteoporosis. Some studies have shown that soya bean products can help to alleviate post-menopausal symptoms and lower blood cholesterol levels.

beansprouts

Packed with nutrients, beansprouts are the shoots of sprouting beans, produced when beans are soaked in water, then left in a warm, dark environment to germinate. As the beans grow, the starches, oils and other nutrients they contain are converted into vitamins, enzymes and proteins, minerals and sugars. In particular, levels of vitamin C and the B vitamins thiamin, folate, B_6 and biotin increase dramatically. As a result, beansprouts are a valuable source of these vitamins as well as providing easy-to-digest protein. They are also low in calories.

raspberries

Like all berry fruits, raspberries are an excellent source of vitamin C, needed to make the protein collagen (for healthy teeth, bones and skin). Vitamin C also aids the absorption of iron from vegetables and acts as an antioxidant in the body, neutralising the unstable molecules (free radicals) that may eventually lead to cancer. A handful of raspberries supplies about half an adult's daily requirement of vitamin C.

Raspberries contain some vitamin E, which also acts as an antioxidant in the body, and folate (which is required for cell division and healthy red blood cells). They contain fibre, too, and the mineral potassium. At only 25 Calories per 100g (3½oz) portion, raspberries are a nutritious choice for those on a low-calorie diet.

As raspberries have only a short shelf-life, vitamin losses due to storage are minimal. Canned raspberries, however, have lower levels of nutrients than the fresh fruit and a high proportion of added sugar. Frozen raspberries are a healthier alternative when the fresh fruit is out of season, as most nutrients survive freezing.

benefits

1 **Good source of vitamin C.**

2 **Contain folate, potassium and fibre.**

rheumatoid arthritis

This condition is a chronic inflammation of the joints, causing severe joint damage and disability. It affects about 2 per cent of the population worldwide, and is much more common in women than in men. It often starts between the ages of 30 and 40, although it can also strike children, teenagers and the elderly.

Many experts believe it is an autoimmune disease, which arises when the body's immune system malfunctions and attacks healthy joints. Although most sufferers require drug treatment, there is evidence that diet can also help. Some nutritionists recommend three portions of oil-rich fish a week: fish such as salmon, fresh tuna, trout and sardines contain omega-3 fatty acids, which have anti-inflammatory properties.

Some people find that a food allergy aggravates their condition. A variety of foods have been implicated, including milk and milk products, corn and cereals. If you suspect a food allergy, consult your doctor before eliminating any food from your diet. Studies have found that a vegetarian diet can sometimes alleviate symptoms.

eat more

Oil-rich fish such as mackerel, sardines, salmon, trout and fresh tuna, for omega-3 fatty acids, which have anti-inflammatory properties.

Stewed rhubarb is a good source of potassium, the mineral needed to maintain a healthy fluid balance in the body.

rhubarb

Although classified as a vegetable, rhubarb is used as a fruit, requiring plenty of sugar to mask the characteristic sourness caused by its high acid content. Apart from large amounts of malic and citric acids, rhubarb also contains oxalic acid, which inhibits the absorption of iron and calcium. Oxalic acid can aggravate joint problems in people with gout or arthritis, and lead to kidney stones in susceptible people. If you suffer from any of these conditions, avoid rhubarb and other rich sources of oxalic acid, such as beetroot, tea, peanuts and chocolate. Rhubarb leaves are poisonous, containing a much larger proportion of oxalic acid than the edible stalks.

Stewed rhubarb is a good source of potassium, needed for a healthy fluid balance in the body. It also contains small amounts of vitamin C. Although rhubarb is naturally low in calories, stewing it with sugar will increase its energy content markedly. Avoid cooking rhubarb in aluminium pans, as the acids can react with the metal on the pan surface, causing it to leach into the stewed fruit.

benefit

Good source of potassium.

drawbacks

1 **Contains oxalic acid, which inhibits calcium and iron absorption.**

2 **Oxalic acid may promote the formation of kidney stones.**

3 **Rhubarb leaves are highly poisonous.**

rice

Like most cereals, rice is a good source of energy, containing a large amount of starch. It is a staple food in many parts of the world, supplying protein, fibre, vitamins and minerals. However, as with all grains, removing the bran layers and the germ substantially reduces nutrient levels. Polished white rice contains far less fibre and B vitamins (such as thiamin, riboflavin and niacin) than brown rice. The thiamin content can drop by 80 per cent, so thiamin deficiency tends to be common in populations whose consumption of white rice is high. One way to reduce loss of B vitamins is by parboiling rice before milling. This causes some of the B vitamins to seep into the grain, resulting in the much more nutritious 'easy-cook' rice.

Although brown rice may seem the best option, it is not suitable for everyone. Its high phytic acid content inhibits the absorption of iron and calcium in the gut, so it is best avoided by those prone to deficiencies of these minerals. Rice is a safe alternative for people with COELIAC DISEASE who are sensitive to the gluten in wheat.

benefits

1 **Good source of energy.**

2 **Suitable for people with coeliac disease.**

3 **Brown rice is a good source of B vitamins.**

drawback

Brown rice contains phytic acid, which reduces iron and calcium absorption in the gut.

Many everyday foods contain 'hidden' salt, and too much of it can cause high blood pressure

salt and sodium

benefits

1 Help to regulate the body's fluid balance and blood pressure.

2 Enhance the flavour of foods.

drawbacks

1 A high intake raises blood pressure and may lead to heart disease, stroke or kidney failure.

2 A high intake encourages calcium excretion and increases the risk of osteoporosis.

Most of us eat too much salt (sodium chloride). In Britain, the average adult intake is 9g a day, although the World Health Organisation recommends no more than 6g a day. Too much salt can lead to fluid retention and high BLOOD PRESSURE, which in turn may result in heart disease, stroke or kidney failure.

However, with no sodium at all, our cells, nerves and muscles could not function properly. Sodium also works together with potassium to regulate our body fluids and to maintain a healthy blood pressure. Individual requirements depend on age and how much is lost through sweating. Most adults need about 1,600mg of sodium a day – the equivalent of about 4g of salt (less than one level teaspoon) – and can excrete any excess. But in babies and young children, who are less efficient at excretion, excess sodium can cause dehydration, which in rare instances can be fatal.

Most adults need less than one level teaspoon of salt a day.

About one-fifth of our sodium intake comes from the salt we add to food. Sodium that occurs naturally in fruit, vegetables, meat, fish, grains and pulses accounts for another fifth. But 60 per cent of the sodium in our diet comes from manufactured foods that contain salt or sodium compounds, such as sodium nitrate, monosodium glutamate or sodium bicarbonate. To reduce sodium intake, eat fewer PROCESSED FOODS and more fresh foods. Gradually stop adding salt in cooking or at the table, and substitute herbs or spices for flavour. Low-sodium salt (50:50 sodium and potassium) is now widely available but is unsuitable for diabetics or anyone with kidney disease.

Sweet, juicy and easy to peel, these small orange citrus fruits can help to protect against winter colds

satsumas and tangerines

Native to the Far East, both satsumas and tangerines are available throughout the year but are at their most flavoursome during the winter months. They are especially valuable to us at this time of year because they are a good source of vitamin C, which the body needs to fight infections such as colds and flu. Their nutrient value is very similar: one satsuma or tangerine supplies about three-quarters of the adult daily requirement of vitamin C, and contains around 30 Calories.

These bright orange fruits also provide us with some beta carotene, the plant form of vitamin A. We need this antioxidant vitamin to fight infection and for good vision and healthy skin. They supply folate, too, which our bodies need to make the genetic material DNA, and for cell division. In addition, they supply potassium, the mineral that helps to regulate blood pressure and the body's fluid levels.

Surprisingly, the membranes that surround each segment of fruit and the fluffy pith are also nutritionally valuable. Both of them contain pectin (which is also found in apples and some other fruits), a form of soluble fibre that is believed to help reduce blood cholesterol levels (a big contributor to heart disease and stroke). The membranes and pith contain bioflavonoids, which act as ANTIOXIDANTS, helping to ward off certain cancers.

When buying satsumas and tangerines, choose those with glossy, deep orange skins. The juiciest fruits are those that are relatively heavy for their size.

The membrane surrounding each segment contains fibre that may help reduce blood cholesterol.

benefits

1 **Good sources of vitamin C.**

2 **Contain beta carotene and folate, and provide potassium for healthy blood pressure.**

3 **Membranes and pith contain pectin, which may help to lower blood cholesterol levels.**

Choosing sauces carefully makes it possible to give extra flavour to meals without adding a lot of fat or sodium

sauces and dressings

Some sauces affect the fat content of a meal dramatically. The main ingredients of hollandaise sauce, for example, are egg yolks and butter, making it extremely high in saturated FATS; carbonara sauce is also high in fat – in addition to egg yolks and cream, it contains bacon and Parmesan cheese. White sauces, by contrast, are relatively low in fat, especially if they are made with semi-skimmed or skimmed milk.

Some types, such as soya sauce and many Chinese and Indian ready-to-use sauces, are high in sodium, so they should not be eaten too often. When they are used, no extra salt is required. Redcurrant jelly and other fruity condiments are high in sugar so should be used sparingly.

Many condiments and sauces are consumed in such small amounts as to contribute few useful nutrients to the average daily diet. Tomato ketchup, however, provides the body with lycopene, a carotenoid pigment that may help to protect against certain forms of cancer.

Many dressings, including mayonnaise, are relatively high in fat. The major ingredient, alongside vinegar and flavourings (such as black pepper, mustard or herbs) is usually a vegetable oil of some kind. Vegetable oils are generally high in unsaturated fats, either monounsaturates (such as olive oil) or polyunsaturates (such as sunflower oil). Although these are preferable to saturated fats, intake should still be limited.

Low-fat or reduced-fat dressings are now widely available. As an alternative, a little water can be added to homemade oil and vinegar dressings. A dessertspoon of dressing should be ample for a portion of salad.

benefit

Add flavour and interest to food.

drawbacks

1 Many classic sauces are high in fat.

2 Soya sauce and some Indian and Chinese ready-to-use sauces are high in sodium.

sausages and salami

Most sausages tend to be less nutritious than fresh meat, but they contain the same range of nutrients. They are generally high in fat (and therefore calories) and salt, but they do provide protein. Strict rules govern their meat content. An ordinary 'pork sausage', for example, must have at least 65 per cent pork meat alongside fillers such as breadcrumbs or biscuit.

Weight for weight, salami usually contains more protein than other types of sausage, but the drawback is that it is packed with fat and sodium. A 100g (3½oz) portion of salami supplies more sodium than an adult needs in a day. Frankfurters (which have half as much fat and salt), salami and other smoked sausages may contain tyramine, which could trigger an allergic reaction in some people.

Vegetarian sausages are made with protein (often soya or peanuts), vegetable fat, grains and flavourings. They contain more fibre than their meat equivalents, slightly less fat (most of which is unsaturated) and a lot less sodium. However, they do not supply as much iron, zinc and vitamin B_{12}.

benefits

Good sources of energy and protein.

drawbacks

1 High fat and salt content.

2 Salami and other smoked sausages may trigger allergies in susceptible people.

seaweed

An everyday food in the Japanese diet, seaweed is increasingly valued in the West for its health benefits and subtle flavours. Many oriental varieties, including arame, kombu, wakame and nori, are now available in health food shops, along with laver and other seaweeds from Britain's shores.

Most seaweeds are an excellent source of iodine. This mineral is essential for a healthy thyroid gland, which regulates the body's metabolism, growth and development. Other minerals found in seaweeds are: potassium for a healthy heartbeat and fluid balance, calcium for strong bones, magnesium for healthy muscle and nerve function, iron and copper for healthy blood, and zinc for the immune system.

Seaweeds contain several B vitamins and some varieties are virtually the only plant sources of vitamin B_{12} – though nutritional experts disagree over how easily the body can absorb it. Some also contain beta carotene, which the body converts into vitamin A. The high sodium content of some types of seaweed makes them unsuitable for anyone following a low-salt diet.

benefit

1 Most types are an excellent source of iodine.

2 Supplies a range of minerals.

3 Contains B vitamins, including vitamin B_{12}, as well as beta carotene.

drawback

Some types are high in sodium.

sex drive

eat more

Oysters, and other zinc-rich foods, which are essential for fertility.

cut down on

1 Drinks containing caffeine or alcohol, which may reduce sex drive.

2 Smoking, which can lead to atherosclerosis and impotence.

A balanced diet, regular exercise and low stress levels all contribute to a healthy sex drive. Men concerned that their libido is low should include zinc-rich foods in their diet. They need zinc for the development of the reproductive organs and for sperm production; a lack of it can cause infertility and impotence. Oysters are an excellent source of zinc. Other good sources include red meat and pumpkin seeds.

Some people find that vitamin E-rich foods, such as eggs and wheatgerm, help to maintain a healthy sex drive but there is still no scientific evidence to support this. Stress is known to suppress sex drive, as is too much alcohol or nicotine. Smoking also increases the risk of atherosclerosis (furring up of the arteries). When this affects the penile artery it can lead to impotence in older men. To reduce the risk, stop smoking and try to include plenty of antioxidant-rich foods in your diet.

The caffeine contained in coffee, tea and plain chocolate can also reduce sex drive in some people. High cholesterol levels or blood pressure can have a similar effect.

shellfish

benefits

1 Rich in minerals and an abundant source of B vitamins, especially B_{12}.

2 Good source of omega-3 fatty acids.

drawbacks

1 Prone to bacterial contamination.

2 May trigger allergic reactions in susceptible people.

3 Contains purines, which aggravate gout.

Crustaceans (lobster, crab and prawns), molluscs (oysters, mussels and scallops) and cephalopods (squid and octopus) are all types of shellfish. Low in fat and high in protein, most supply: abundant vitamin B_{12}, needed for the formation of red blood cells and for healthy nerves; zinc, vital for wound healing and the development of reproductive organs; and selenium, an antioxidant that may ward off cancer.

Many shellfish, like oil-rich fish, contain omega-3 fatty acids. These are thought to protect against both heart and circulation

problems. Some shellfish, such as mussels, also contain iodine, needed for the efficient functioning of the thyroid gland, which controls the body's metabolic rate.

Certain varieties of shellfish, notably shrimps, prawns and crayfish, are high in dietary CHOLESTEROL. However, recent studies have shown they also contain a substance that lowers blood cholesterol, which may help reduce the risk of heart disease.

All shellfish are highly perishable and prone to bacterial contamination. Always buy them fresh and from reputable sources. Because molluscs are filter feeders, they collect any pollution in the water in their tissues. The safest shellfish to eat are those farmed commercially in clean waters. Supermarkets and all good fishmongers will only buy shellfish from seas that are certified as being the cleanest. The livers of lobsters and crabs filter toxins, so avoid the green 'tomally' in lobsters and the yellow 'mustard' in crabs.

People with GOUT should cut down on shellfish: they tend to be high in purines, chemicals that trigger a build-up of uric acid crystals in the joints, causing inflammation. In susceptible people, shellfish can trigger allergic responses, including nettle rash or hives (urticaria).

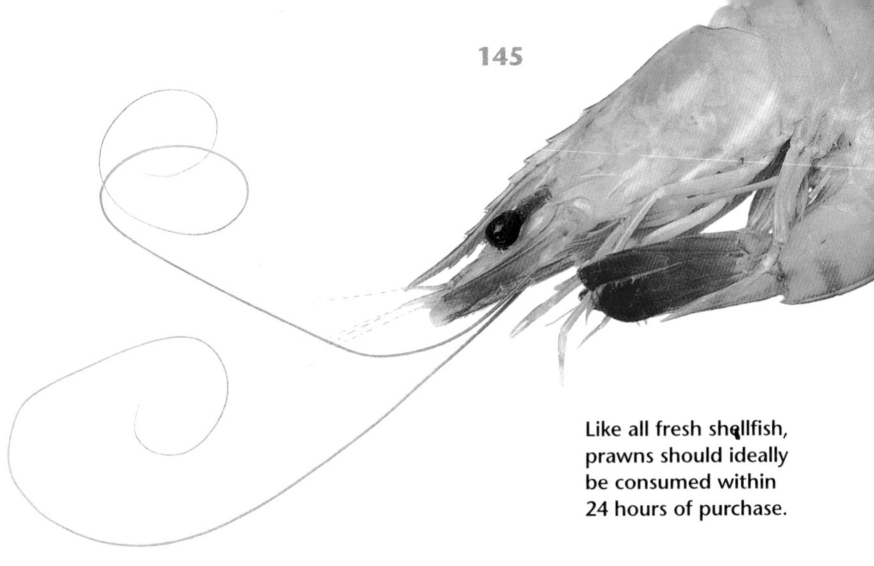

Like all fresh shellfish, prawns should ideally be consumed within 24 hours of purchase.

what's in shellfish?

type of shellfish	protein (g)	fat (g)	minerals	vitamins
MUSSELS BOILED	17	2	Rich in iron and iodine; good source of selenium.	Excellent source of vitamin B_{12}; useful source of riboflavin and vitamin E.
OYSTERS RAW	15	15	Excellent source of zinc and copper; good source of iron and potassium; contain selenium.	Excellent source of vitamin B_{12}; contain niacin, vitamin E, thiamin and riboflavin.
SCALLOPS STEAMED	23	1.4	Rich in selenium; good source of potassium; contain zinc.	Excellent source of vitamin B_{12}; useful source of niacin.
CRAB BOILED	20	5	Good source of zinc and potassium; contains magnesium.	Good source of riboflavin; useful source of pantothenic acid; contains vitamin B_6.
LOBSTER BOILED	22	3.5	Excellent source of selenium; useful source of zinc.	Excellent source of vitamin B_{12}; useful source of niacin.
PRAWNS BOILED	23	2	Useful source of selenium; contain iodine.	Excellent source of vitamin B_{12}.
SQUID RAW	13	1.5	Excellent source of selenium; contains iodine.	Excellent source of vitamin B_{12}; good source of vitamin B_6; useful source of vitamin E.

Nutrients and comparisons are per 100g (3½oz).

sinusitis

eat more

1 Decongestant foods, such as chillies, garlic, ginger and horseradish.

2 Shellfish and nuts for zinc, and citrus fruit for vitamin C, to boost the immune system.

cut down on

Dairy products, which may suppress the production of decongesting secretions in susceptible people.

The sinuses are air-filled cavities that drain into the nose. They are kept healthy by a watery mucus that protects their delicate membrane lining. However, if the lining is infected by a cold virus it becomes inflamed, blocking up the nasal passages through which mucus normally drains and producing a thicker, infected mucus known as catarrh. Sufferers often experience an aching face and a 'bunged-up' feeling.

If caused by a cold, these symptoms disappear with the cold after a week or so, but acute sinusitis that is connected to an infection such as tonsillitis may last longer, persisting as chronic sinusitis. Chronic conditions (characterised by a streaming nose and sounding blocked up) can also be the result of ALLERGIES, in which case dairy products are common culprits. Consult your doctor for a diagnosis.

Foods that are natural decongestants are especially valuable for relieving sinusitis. Chillies and ginger increase mucus flow and help to clear congested airways. Garlic and onion, horseradish, cloves and cinnamon have similarly beneficial powers.

skin problems

eat more

1 For acne: nuts, pumpkin seeds and lean lamb to supply zinc; fruit and vegetables for vitamin C; spinach, carrots and mangoes for vitamin A; sunflower seeds and avocados for vitamin E.

2 For eczema: zinc-rich foods (see above).

3 For psoriasis: 3-7 portions a week of oil-rich fish.

Skin complaints, such as acne, eczema and psoriasis, often cause emotional as well as physical scarring. However, symptoms can usually be relieved significantly by making a few simple dietary changes.

Although acne is most common among teenagers, it can strike as late as middle age. Hormonal imbalances and stress lead to pores becoming clogged with excess sebum, resulting in unsightly spots.

Anyone suffering from acne should try to limit their intake of sweets, fizzy drinks and fatty foods, particularly salty crisps and chips, which aggravate the condition in some people. Be sure to have a nutritious diet that supplies all the vital vitamins and minerals, especially zinc (which some sufferers tend to lack) and vitamins A and E.

Eczema – red, itchy, dry and flaky skin that may bleed or blister – is often brought on by allergens. Contact eczema develops on skin sensitive to external irritants, such as wool, metal, detergents or onions. Atopic eczema often affects people with a family history of asthma or hay fever, and sensitivity to certain foods is frequently the cause. A medically supervised exclusion diet can identify the trigger; if symptoms abate when a food is avoided but recur when it is reintroduced, that food is probably the culprit. Well-known allergens are milk, eggs, fish, shellfish, tomatoes, nuts and wheat.

Psoriasis is a chronic disorder characterised by scaly red patches that tend to appear on the elbows, knees and scalp and which may bleed or become infected. While there is no cure, nutritional therapies can have beneficial results. Eating oil-rich fish (herring, mackerel, salmon, tuna) once a day has been found to bring about a remarkable improvement in some people and even less frequent helpings can give considerable relief; the omega-3 fatty acids present in oil-rich fish are known to have anti-inflammatory powers. Sunlight seems to relieve the symptoms, and sometimes exposed skin will clear up spontaneously during the summer months.

Drinking 2.5 litres (4½ pints) of water a day will help all sufferers to improve the general condition of their skin, by flushing out the body's waste products.

cut down on

1 For acne: sweets and salty snacks.

2 For eczema: known food triggers, which might include milk, eggs, nuts and wheat.

drink more

Water, to relieve all types of skin condition.

sleep

Our eating habits can affect how well we sleep. A large meal eaten late at night often interferes with sleep, particularly if it contains rich or spicy foods, which can cause indigestion. But going to bed hungry is also a reason for poor sleep; people on low-calorie diets often find it difficult to fall asleep and may wake in the night. The caffeine contained in coffee, tea, cola and plain chocolate can cause sleeplessness if consumed during the evening. A few drinks with dinner often help to induce sleep, but too many will have the opposite effect. Certain foods may improve the chances of a good night's sleep. A sweet, milky drink can promote sleep because the sugar it contains enhances the uptake of tryptophan from the bloodstream into the brain. Tryptophan is crucial for the synthesis of serotonin, a brain chemical needed for normal sleep. Starchy foods, such as pasta, rice and potatoes, can have a similiar effect.

Herbal teas such as valerian and camomile may help to fight insomnia. Some naturopaths suggest adding honey, which they claim is a mild sedative.

eat more

Starchy foods, such as bread and potatoes.

drink more

Sweet, milky drinks just before bedtime.

avoid

1 Large meals late in the evening.

2 Rich or spicy foods, which cause indigestion.

3 Caffeine, found in coffee, tea and cola.

smoked and cured food

benefit

As methods of preserving food, curing and smoking help to prevent food poisoning.

drawbacks

1 High salt content.

2 Smoked foods contain compounds that may be carcinogenic if eaten in excess.

Salting, smoking and drying are all traditional methods of preserving foods. Apart from preventing deterioration, these processes also impart distinctive flavours. Smoke contains more than 200 chemicals, some of which are toxic to bacteria. Others are carcinogenic. In some parts of the world, such as Scandinavia, a high incidence of stomach cancer has been linked to the consumption of large amounts of smoked fish. However, in Britain most people do not eat enough smoked foods to justify any concern about potential risks.

Apart from their high salt content, most smoked and cured foods also contain small amounts of nitrite and nitrate. These preservatives give cooked meats an attractive pink colour and, more importantly, inhibit growth of bacteria responsible for botulism (see FOOD POISONING). However, in some preliminary laboratory experiments, nitrites reacted with foods to form carcinogenic substances. Although there is no evidence of this effect in humans, nitrite levels in food are still carefully monitored and kept to a minimum by manufacturers.

smoking and diet

eat more

1 Fresh fruit and vegetables for vitamin C and other antioxidants.

2 Avocados, nuts, seeds and vegetable oils, for vitamin E.

3 Oil-rich fish for omega-3 fatty acids.

avoid

1 Foods high in saturated fats.

2 Supplements that contain beta carotene.

The best way of preventing the chronic illnesses associated with smoking is to kick the habit. In Britain, about half of those who smoke regularly will die from it.

If you do smoke, increase your intake of antioxidant vitamins by eating more fresh fruit and vegetables (for vitamin C, other antioxidants and flavonoids), and avocados, vegetable oils, and nuts (for vitamin E). Antioxidant vitamins help to neutralise the harmful free radicals found in tobacco smoke. Smokers need twice as much vitamin C in their diet as non-smokers, since their bodies use it up faster. Supplements can boost your intake of antioxidant vitamins, but avoid those containing high levels of synthetic beta carotene, as they may raise the risk of lung cancer in smokers.

Smoking increases the tendency of the blood to clot, making a heart attack or stroke more likely. A diet that is low in saturated fat, and high in fibre and oil-rich fish (for omega-3 fatty acids) can help to reduce the risk. Lycopene (the red pigment found in tomato products) may even help to reverse smoke-damage to lungs.

Most fizzy drinks and squashes supply energy but few nutrients

soft drinks

With water and sugar as their main components, most soft drinks have limited nutritional benefits. Although they provide instant energy, they are high in calories. Their high sugar content (a 330ml can of lemonade contains about four teaspoons of sugar; a can of cola about seven) contributes to tooth decay, particularly in children. So soft drinks should be drunk only at mealtimes, rather than throughout the day. Sugar-free versions, made with artificial sweeteners such as saccharin and aspartame, do not contribute to tooth decay and are almost calorie-free. But some naturopaths claim they can have adverse side effects and are best avoided. Many cola drinks contain phosphoric acid, which may reduce absorption of calcium (essential for healthy teeth and bones). Cola drinks also contain caffeine (about a third of the amount in a cup of coffee), but decaffeinated versions are now available.

Low-calorie varieties aside, squashes are also high in sugar – up to eight teaspoons in 300ml – though some are rich in vitamin C: 300ml of blackcurrant squash supplies up to 1½ times the adult daily requirement.

benefits

1 Good source of energy.

2 Some squashes are an excellent source of vitamin C.

drawbacks

1 Can be high in sugar, leading to tooth decay.

2 Cola drinks contain caffeine, which in excess can cause palpitations.

3 Many cola drinks contain phosphoric acid, which inhibits calcium absorption.

food note

Fruit juices – such as orange, apple and cranberry – can be a good source of vitamin C, since most of the nutrient is retained in the extracting process. However, juices tend to be high in sugar and can therefore contribute to tooth decay.

soups

benefit

Depending on their ingredients, soups can supply protein, fibre and most vitamins and minerals.

drawbacks

1 **Commercial varieties can be high in sodium.**

2 **Canned soups lose some vitamin C in processing.**

Homemade soups can be highly nutritious if made with lots of vegetables, since most of the nutrients that leach into the water during cooking are retained. Additional ingredients such as meat and pulses will supply extra protein, fibre and B vitamins. Milk and cream will add calcium, but they will also increase the fat content.

A good stock, based on vegetables and meat or fish bones and trimmings, forms the base of many soups. Although stocks usually take a while to make, they can be made in large batches, then frozen and used as needed. Alternatively, fresh stock in a range of flavours is available from many supermarkets. Stock cubes are another option, although they contain ADDITIVES and tend to be high in sodium.

Canned soups are sterilised, a process that destroys some nutrients such as vitamin C. Carton soups are healthier because they are pasteurised, a process that retains most nutrients. However, both types tend to be high in salt. Dried packet soups are the least nutritious, containing colourings, flavourings and thickeners.

spices

food note

In traditional medicine, ginger is often prescribed to relieve nausea, particularly morning and travel sickness. Add a pinch or two of grated fresh ginger to a hot drink, or take a tablet (available at most health food shops) with a glass of water.

With their capacity to transform the flavour and colour of all kinds of food, spices are used in cooking all over the world. Some, such as cinnamon, cloves, ginger, nutmeg and pepper, originate from the tropical regions of Asia. While others, including fennel, fenugreek and mustard, are found throughout the Mediterranean. Juniper berries and caraway seeds grow in the cooler regions of northern Europe.

Nutritionally, spices do not contribute significantly to the diet because they tend to be used in small amounts. However, varieties such as chilli powder and paprika are extremely rich in beta carotene. Many spices also contain B vitamins, potassium, calcium and iron, as well as natural toxins. Nutmeg, mace and black pepper, for example, are a source of myristicin, which has mild sedative and anaesthetic properties but which is toxic if consumed in large quantities. Other spices, such as red star anise, contain compounds known to cause cancer in animals. However, there is no evidence that spices are harmful at the levels at which we consume them.

spinach

Although spinach is not as rich in iron as it is widely believed to be, it remains one of the most nutritious vegetables, especially when eaten raw. It is an exceptionally good source of beta carotene and provides vitamins C and E, all of which are antioxidants that protect against cancer, strokes and heart disease. The specific carotenes that it contains are thought to help prevent deterioration of the centre of the retina, a common cause of blindness in the elderly. Spinach is also a valuable source of folic acid, and a useful source of calcium and potassium, as well as iron. Unfortunately, its high levels of oxalic acid bond with both calcium and iron and hamper the body's absorption of these vital minerals. Eating spinach with vegetables high in vitamin C (such as potatoes) will maximise the amount of iron absorbed from it.

benefits

1 Excellent source of cancer-fighting antioxidant vitamins.

2 Good source of folic acid and a useful source of calcium, potassium and iron.

drawback

Oxalic acid in spinach limits absorption of calcium and iron, and can encourage kidney-stone formation in susceptible people.

squashes and pumpkins

Although they are favourites in American and Caribbean kitchens, pumpkins are more often associated with Hallowe'en lanterns in Britain, and deserve greater popularity. So do their close relatives the winter squashes – of which acorn, butternut and kabocha are among the best known of many varieties.

Their bright yellow or orange flesh is a clue to the nutritional riches that squashes and pumpkins contain: all varieties are rich in beta carotene, the plant form of vitamin A. As a result, they can be especially useful in vegan and vegetarian diets, which lack animal sources of vitamin A. As they also contain vitamins C and E, and flavonoids, pumpkins and squashes are an excellent source of antioxidants, protecting against damage to cells by free radicals, which can lead to cancer and heart disease.

Pumpkin seeds are one of the most nutritious foods of all. As well as providing vitamin E, they are packed with zinc, iron, potassium, magnesium and phosphorus. They make a highly nutritious snack and can be easily incorporated into salads.

benefits

1 Rich in beta carotene and contain vitamins C and E and flavonoids.

2 Very low in calories – only 13 per 100g (3½oz) serving.

3 Easily digested and rarely cause allergies, so are ideal for weaning babies.

4 Seeds are rich in vitamin E, zinc, iron and other minerals.

Rich in vitamin C, these scarlet berries may also help to protect against cancer

strawberries

benefits

1 Excellent source of vitamin C.

2 Good source of cancer-fighting antioxidants.

3 Low in calories.

drawbacks

1 Can cause allergic reactions.

2 Seeds can aggravate bowel conditions such as colitis.

One of the most popular summer fruits, strawberries contain more vitamin C than any other berry. A 100g (3½oz) serving of fresh strawberries has only 27 Calories, yet supplies 77mg of vitamin C – more than an adult's daily requirement. Eating them after iron-rich green vegetables such as broccoli, peas and watercress, or adding them to iron-fortified breakfast cereals, will improve the body's absorption of iron.

Strawberries also provide soluble and insoluble fibre, which helps prevent constipation; and recent research suggests that they could be among the top fruits for protecting against cancer, thanks to their antioxidant properties.

Some people should avoid strawberries, though. Occasionally, a substance in the fruit prompts the body to produce an excessive amount of histamine, which causes an itchy rash called hives. Anyone with an intolerance of aspirin, which contains acetylsalicylic acid, should stay away from strawberries as they contain similar substances called salicylates. The seeds may also aggravate certain bowel disorders, such as ulcerative colitis.

One serving of fresh strawberries contains only 27 Calories, yet supplies more vitamin C than an adult's daily requirement.

A healthy diet can help equip your body to cope better with the effects of stress

stress

eat more

Complex carbohydrates – in wholemeal bread, breakfast cereals, pasta, rice and oats – which have a calming effect.

cut down on

Alcohol, smoking and caffeine, all of which can aggravate stress.

health tips

Try to reinforce the benefits of a healthy diet with exercise and periods of relaxation. Aerobic exercise boosts oxygen levels while lowering cholesterol, as well as increasing immunity, energy and a sense of wellbeing. Relaxation techniques – such as deep breathing exercises – may also help to relieve the physical and mental effects of stress.

Faced with stress, our bodies go into 'fight or flight' mode: adrenaline causes blood pressure to rise, blood flows away from the digestive system to muscles, and glucose and fatty acids are released into the blood to fuel muscles. Prolonged stress increases the risk of heart disease because of these raised levels of fats and cholesterol. Other physical consequences include stomach ulcers, migraines, palpitations, indigestion, tenseness, sweating, fatigue and insomnia.

Whatever the cause of stress – from a major blow, such as bereavement, to worry about an impending exam – good nutrition can be a potent antidote. Stress weakens the immune system, leaving the body more vulnerable to infection and illness, and certain nutrients are used up more quickly so it is vital to replace them. Foods rich in B vitamins, for energy and a healthy nervous system, and in vitamin C and zinc for resistance to infection, are crucial. Complex carbohydrates, found in wholemeal bread, pasta and oats, supply energy (essential for those exhausted by stress) and have a calming effect on the brain. Too much caffeine stimulates the nervous system and is likely to have the reverse effect.

case study

Harry visited his GP reporting twitching under his right eye, sweaty palms and shortness of breath. These are all classic symptoms of stress. The doctor suggested he avoid tea, coffee and sugary foods, which can all aggravate stress. He was advised instead to eat frequent, small meals rich in complex carbohydrates, such as bread, rice, oats, pasta and potatoes. These foods give a steady stream of energy that helps reduce the fatigue caused by stress, and they have a calming effect on the brain. Harry was also told to practise a form of relaxed breathing to ease his anxiety.

Sugar comes in many different forms. It is a major source of energy but supplies few useful nutrients

sugar and sweeteners

Simple sugars supply an almost immediate source of energy, being quickly converted to glucose in the body. There are several types apart from sucrose (table sugar), including glucose and fructose (present in honey and fruit), lactose (milk sugar) and maltose (in sprouting wheat and barley). Fructose is the sweetest sugar, followed by sucrose, maltose and glucose, with lactose being the least sweet. Some people are intolerant of lactose because they do not have the enzyme lactase, needed to digest it (see also ALLERGIES).

Sugars are classified as either intrinsic or extrinsic, depending on which foods they come from. Intrinsic sugars are contained within the tissues of plant foods such as fruit and vegetables, while extrinsic sugars are those added to foods or present naturally in honey, milk or fruit juice. Intrinsic sugars are absorbed more slowly by the body, preventing rapid changes in blood sugar levels, because digestive enzymes have to break down the cell walls first.

High intakes of sugar have been blamed for various conditions, including heart disease, diabetes and hyperactivity, but there is no scientific evidence to support such claims. Experts now believe that sugar is not the culprit in obesity and that fat is the more likely villain. However, a high intake of sugar-rich foods such as confectionery, cakes, biscuits and soft drinks is a cause of tooth decay. Nutritionists also worry that eating too many of these can displace more nutritious foods from the diet, such as fruit and vegetables. The Department of Health recommends that extrinsic sugars should make up no more than 10 per cent of total energy intake.

Many foods are now sweetened with artificial sweeteners. Some, such as the sugar alcohols sorbitol and xylitol, are popular in diabetic foods and tooth-friendly chewing gum. They contain as many calories as sugar, but are poorly absorbed in the body, preventing a sharp rise in blood sugar levels. However, a high intake of sugar alcohols can sometimes lead to diarrhoea. Intense sweeteners, such as aspartame and saccharin, are 140–350 times sweeter than sugar. They contain almost no calories but some naturopaths warn they may cause adverse side effects in certain people.

benefits

1 **Many sugars are an instant source of energy.**

2 **Artificial sweeteners are almost calorie-free.**

drawbacks

1 **Too much of most sugars can lead to tooth decay.**

2 **Sugar-rich foods can displace more nutritious foods from the diet.**

3 **Some people are intolerant of lactose (milk sugar).**

There is nothing like a cup of tea to revive your spirits, but could it also protect your health?

tea

benefits

1 **Contains antioxidants that may protect against heart disease.**

2 **Supplies fluoride, to help fight tooth decay.**

drawbacks

1 **Excessive amounts can stain teeth.**

2 **Reduces iron absorption from food.**

3 **May cause gastric irritation.**

Whether you drink Indian or China tea, research suggests that it could be good for your health. Tea contains chemicals (polyphenols and bioflavonoids) that have strong ANTIOXIDANT properties, which some experts suggest may protect against cancer and heart disease. The fluoride in tea may also help reduce tooth decay.

Polyphenols contribute to the colour, flavour and astringency of tea. Collectively known as tannins, they can stain the teeth of heavy tea drinkers and interfere with iron absorption in the body. It is best to avoid drinking tea when eating iron-rich foods such as meat, eggs and green leafy vegetables. Like coffee, tea contains the stimulant caffeine: one cup supplies about 40mg, compared with 60mg in a cup of instant coffee. This can boost mental alertness but in excess it may lead to tremors and palpitations. Strong black tea can stimulate acid secretion in the stomach, causing gastric irritation, especially in those suffering from peptic ulcers.

herbal teas

These teas, made from dried herbs, have become increasingly popular. Many have medicinal properties, but need to be taken regularly to have any significant effect. Here are four of the best known:

Camomile Valued for its soothing, calming effects. May help relieve stress and insomnia.

Elderflower Believed to help cure congestion in those suffering from a cold.

Fennel An old-fashioned remedy for indigestion.

Peppermint Traditionally drunk after dinner, to ease indigestion and wind. Also alleviates nausea.

Pregnant women are advised to stay away from herbal teas, with the exception of mint and camomile. Raspberry leaf tea must be avoided until the final 12 weeks of pregnancy (see HERBS).

thrush

Thrush or candidiasis is a fungal infection triggered by the yeast organism *Candida albicans*. It afflicts mainly the mouth and vagina, and can become a chronic condition for certain susceptible people.

Candida albicans grows naturally on the skin and in the gut, but its numbers are usually kept in check by other colonies of bacteria living in our bodies. If this healthy balance of micro-organisms is disturbed, *Candida albicans* multiplies and causes thrush. This tends to happen when the immune system has been weakened – by an infection (such as flu) or following a long course of broad-spectrum antibiotics, which may destroy protective bacteria.

Vaginal thrush can be treated easily, but a small proportion of women experience recurrent episodes. Claims by alternative therapists that diet can both cause and cure thrush may have some foundation. They advise sufferers to avoid foods containing sugar, yeast, mould or fungi. This means cutting out bread, yeast extract, wine, some cheeses and mushrooms. But care must be taken to maintain a balanced diet.

food note

Most women experience at least one episode of vaginal thrush. Some doctors recommend applying live yogurt to treat it, because this contains the bacterium *Lactobacillus acidophilus*, said to help restore the healthy balance of micro-organisms in the body.

thyroid problems

Located in the front of the neck, the thyroid gland produces iodine-containing hormones responsible for controlling the body's metabolic rate – the speed at which food and oxygen are used up for growth and exercise. Iodine, abundant in fish, seaweed and iodised salt, is essential for the efficient functioning of the thyroid gland. Fortunately, iodine deficiency is rare in the developed world. However, some foods, such as raw cabbage, turnips and swedes, contain goitrogens, substances that can upset thyroid hormone function if eaten in excess when iodine intake is also low. Other causes of thyroid dysfunction include autoimmune disease, when the body's own antibodies attack the thyroid gland. This can lead to hypothyroidism (an underactive thyroid), which slows down metabolism. The symptoms include weight gain and memory loss. Conversely, hyperthyroidism (an overactive thyroid) may develop, causing weight loss, depression and anxiety. Sufferers should increase their intake of energy-rich foods but avoid nicotine and caffeine, which can raise the metabolic rate.

eat more

Energy-rich foods if suffering from hyperthyroidism, to prevent weight loss.

avoid

1 **Raw cabbage, turnips and swedes, which can interfere with thyroid hormone production.**

2 **High-fat foods that promote weight gain (for hypothyroidism).**

3 **Smoking and caffeine (for hyperthyroidism).**

tofu

benefits

1 High in protein.

2 Good source of calcium (if made with calcium sulphate).

3 May protect against certain cancers, heart disease, osteoporosis and menopausal symptoms.

Soya bean curd, or tofu, is produced by curdling soya milk (made from soya beans and water) with a coagulant such as calcium sulphate or magnesium chloride. The resulting firm, cheese-like product can be steamed, fried, baked or grilled. You can also buy silken tofu, which has a creamy consistency suitable for making sauces, dressings and desserts such as ice cream or cheesecake. Both types of tofu are naturally bland, easily absorbing the flavours of other ingredients that they are mixed with, and so are suitable for sweet or savoury dishes. Tofu is rich in protein and low in fat, making it a useful addition to a vegetarian diet. If calcium sulphate is used as a coagulant, tofu is a good source of calcium. It also contains phosphorus, iron, magnesium, some B vitamins and vitamin E. Tofu is low in sodium and calories, although frying significantly increases its calorie content. Like other soya bean-based products, tofu contains phytoestrogens, hormone-like chemicals that may help protect against certain cancers, heart disease, osteoporosis and menopausal symptoms.

tomatoes

benefits

1 May reduce the risk of various cancers.

2 Good source of vitamin C.

drawback

May aggravate eczema or trigger migraine in some people.

Research suggests that eating tomatoes may reduce the risk of certain cancers, particularly those of the prostate, lung and stomach. They contain various beneficial compounds including lycopene, a red carotenoid pigment that may act as an antioxidant in the body. Both fresh and processed tomatoes (especially in tomato ketchup and pasta sauces) contain lycopene. Yet not all tomatoes are red when ripe: some are yellow, while others are purple. These differences in colour are caused by varying levels of carotenoids and the other plant pigments. Like many fruits and vegetables, tomatoes are also a useful source of vitamins C and E. Two medium-sized tomatoes supply half the adult daily requirement of vitamin C. Most experts agree that a diet high in these antioxidant vitamins lowers the risk of certain cancers. Tomatoes are low in calories and also contain folate, potassium and dietary fibre.

Unfortunately, some people cannot tolerate tomatoes. They can aggravate eczema, and green tomatoes may trigger migraines in susceptible people.

Tomatoes contain lycopene, a pigment that may help to protect against prostate cancer. They also supply useful amounts of vitamins C and E.

tooth and gum problems

eat more

1 Dairy products for calcium.

2 Fibrous foods such as apples, particularly after a meal, as they inhibit plaque formation.

cut down on

1 Sweet, sticky foods such as toffee, fudge and dried fruit.

2 Sugary snacks.

3 Acidic and sweet soft drinks and fruit juice.

Tooth decay occurs when bacteria, which are naturally present in the mouth, break down sugars in food to produce acids that dissolve the tooth enamel. Regular brushing and flossing of teeth helps to remove the sticky film, or plaque, which contains colonies of bacteria. Plaque is also one of the major causes of gum disease.

Sugary foods that stick to teeth, such as toffee, fudge and dried fruit, are the main culprits, particularly if eaten between meals. The acids in sweet drinks such as fruit juice, fizzy soft drinks and cordials, also erode tooth enamel. Foods that help to protect teeth against decay include cheese, which increases the flow of saliva and reduces levels of mouth acidity, and fibrous foods such as apples, which have a scouring action that reduces plaque build-up.

In children, healthy tooth formation depends on a good intake of calcium and phosphorus (in milk, yogurt, cheese), magnesium (in wholegrain cereals) and fluoride (in toothpaste, fluoridated tap waters). Vitamin C deficiency can lead to sore gums, so eat plenty of fruit and vegetables.

travelling abroad

safety first

1 Drink boiled or bottled water.

2 Do not take ice in drinks.

3 Avoid salads and any foods washed in local water, and drinks diluted with water.

4 Avoid shellfish, raw fish, and undercooked or lukewarm foods.

5 Avoid any foods from dubious sources.

Trying local delicacies and unusual dishes is part of the joy of travelling, but because hygiene and sanitation may be poor in some areas, it is always advisable to take a few simple precautions.

Remember that in hot climates you will need to drink more water than usual to prevent dehydration, as the body loses more fluids through sweating. Drink boiled or bottled water (use it for brushing teeth, too), and never take ice in drinks, or have squashes that may have been diluted with tap water. Peel fruit and avoid salads that have been washed in local water. Any food from unreliable sources, such as street vendors or market stalls, carries risks, as do foods that may have been undercooked, kept warm for hours or exposed to flies.

Fish and shellfish are best avoided, except in reputable restaurants and hotels; the same holds for steak tartare, beefburgers and pork products, which could harbour tapeworms in certain regions.

Vigilance and common sense should protect you from most potential hazards. If in any doubt about a food or drink, avoid it.

Some foods can aggravate both peptic and mouth ulcers; others can promote healing

ulcers

Peptic ulcers are a very common problem in this country. They occur when the lining of the stomach or duodenum (the section of intestine below the stomach) erodes, causing burning pain, and in severe cases bleeding, vomiting and weight loss. People who have ulcers secrete more stomach acid but less of the protective mucus that lines the stomach. Smoking and a stressful lifestyle are associated with increased risk; however, most experts now believe that ulcers are caused by a bacterial infection, and the culprit is *Helicobacter pylori*.

Although peptic ulcers are effectively treated with drugs, including antibiotics to eliminate *Helicobacter pylori*, diet can also help the healing process. If you have an ulcer, avoid eating large meals and limit your intake of alcohol and caffeine, which can increase acid secretion and irritate the stomach lining. Traditional bland diets prescribed to ulcer patients in the past have been shown to be ineffective. These diets, based on milk products, poached white fish and mashed potatoes, were often high in saturated fats and low in some of the nutrients necessary for wound healing (iron and vitamin C). Ulcer patients are now advised to eat normally and only avoid foods that worsen their symptoms. Pickles, olives, fried foods, onions and spices are common culprits. Some studies suggest a diet high in polyunsaturated fats may protect against certain types of ulcer (possibly by inhibiting the growth of *Helicobacter pylori*), but the evidence is still inconclusive.

Mouth ulcers are painful, inflamed white spots that can occur anywhere in the mouth and usually take about a week to heal. Doctors still do not know what causes them, but emotional stress, mouth injury and, in some women, hormone fluctuations are all thought to play a role. Mouth ulcers have also been linked with diseases of the digestive system, such as CROHN'S DISEASE, ulcerative colitis and COELIAC DISEASE. In elderly people, they may be caused by lack of nutrients, such as iron and folate (found in meat and dark green vegetables) and vitamin B_{12} (found in offal, meat and eggs). If you suffer from mouth ulcers, avoid crisps and other crunchy foods, and salty and acidic foods such as pickles, which irritate the mouth.

eat more

For mouth ulcers:

Meat, offal and dark green vegetables for iron, folate and vitamin B_{12}.

avoid

For peptic ulcers:

1 Caffeine and alcohol.

2 Large meals.

3 Foods that may aggravate symptoms, such as spices, pickles and fried foods.

For mouth ulcers:

Salty and acidic foods such as pickles.

Excluding animal products from your diet can be a healthy choice, but there are possible pitfalls, too

vegetarian and vegan diets

benefits

1 Can lower blood cholesterol, reducing the risk of heart disease.

2 Eating no meat and more foods from plant sources reduces the risk of cancer.

3 A diet high in fibre means less risk of bowel disease.

drawback

Can be low in iron, calcium, zinc, and vitamin B_{12}.

As well as avoiding red meat, vegetarians do not eat poultry or fish. Vegans eat only plant-derived foods, which excludes eggs and dairy products, too.

By cutting out animal products, both groups reduce the amount of saturated fat in their diet. As a result they tend to be slimmer than meat-eaters. They also have less blood cholesterol, which means they are less likely to suffer from heart disease.

Since a high-fat diet is associated with some cancers, cutting out meat may reduce the risk of developing this disease, too. Indeed, studies over the past decade have shown that vegetarians are about 40 per cent less likely to develop cancer in early life than meat-eaters. However, this statistic may be attributable to a high intake of fresh fruit and vegetables, which are rich in ANTIOXIDANT vitamins, rather than to the absence of meat in the diet.

Vegetarians and vegans also eat more fibre than meat-eaters, because their diet usually includes more wholegrain cereals and pulses. This may help reduce the risk of bowel disorders, including colon cancer.

case study

Cutting out animal protein and dairy products can often improve life for people with rheumatoid arthritis. Pat, aged 45, has been on a vegan diet for almost a year and is delighted at the improvement in her condition. To ensure she still gets adequate protein, she eats plenty of pulses, nuts and seeds. Some of these, such as soya beans, walnuts, and pumpkin and sesame seeds, are important sources of omega-3 fatty acids (usually supplied by oil-rich fish in non-vegetarian diets). These are particularly valuable for arthritis sufferers, since they have an anti-inflammatory effect.

To enjoy all these benefits, it is vital to adopt a balanced diet, based on complex carbohydrates, such as wholemeal bread and potatoes, alongside a range of vegetables, fruit, pulses and nuts. The elimination of animal foods can lead to vitamin and mineral deficiencies, notably of vitamin B_{12}, iron, calcium and zinc. So it's vital to include sources of all these nutrients in the diet (see chart). Iron-rich foods, such as dark green vegetables, should be eaten with vitamin C-rich foods, such as orange juice. This will boost absorption of the mineral and help protect against iron-deficiency ANAEMIA. Other key nutrients that vegetarians may lack are iodine and riboflavin.

Provided a vegetarian or vegan diet is well rounded, it should supply adequate protein for all the body's needs. Since only a few sources of plant-derived proteins (for example, soya bean products) supply sufficient amounts of the full range of essential amino acids, a healthy diet should include a variety of cereals and pulses. For young children, cereals and pulses should be combined in the same meal; other people can be a little more flexible.

A vegan diet may not provide sufficient calcium and vitamin B_{12} for pregnant women. A supplement may be necessary, but this should only be taken following consultation with a doctor.

eat more

1 **Iron-rich foods, such as egg yolks, green leafy vegetables and pulses.**

2 **Foods rich in calcium and vitamin B_{12}, such as dairy foods or fortified cereal and soya bean products.**

3 **Foods containing zinc, such as wholegrain cereals and pulses.**

4 **Sources of iodine (seaweed and iodised table salt) and riboflavin (milk, yogurt and fortified breakfast cereals).**

nutrients to keep an eye on

nutrient	what it does	found in
CALCIUM	Needed for the development and maintenance of strong bones and teeth. Also involved in nerve transmission, blood clotting and muscle function.	Milk and dairy products, fortified soya products including tofu, nuts (especially almonds), dark green leafy vegetables, sesame seeds and sunflower seeds.
IRON	An essential component of haemoglobin in red blood cells. Also involved in energy metabolism.	Egg yolks, dark green leafy vegetables, beans and lentils, iron-fortified cereals, wholemeal flour, oatmeal, nuts and parsley.
ZINC	Vital for normal growth and development. Also important for a healthy immune system.	Wholegrain cereals, pulses, peanuts and pumpkin seeds.
VITAMIN B_{12}	Vital for making DNA and myelin, the white sheath that surrounds nerve fibres. Also needed for cell division.	Milk and dairy products, eggs, fortified foods including soya milk and breakfast cereals, and yeast extract.

Although we only need them in minute amounts, vitamins are essential for our bodies to work properly

vitamins

eat more

1 **Offal, especially liver (unless you are pregnant) which contains vitamin A, all the B complex vitamins and vitamin E.**

2 **Oil-rich fish, such as herring, kippers and mackerel, which are full of vitamins A, B_3, B_6, B_{12}, biotin and vitamin E.**

3 **Fruit and vegetables, which are good sources of vitamin C.**

4 **Red, yellow and orange-coloured fruit and vegetables, which contain beta carotene, the plant form of vitamin A.**

5 **Wheatgerm and cereals, which contain vitamins B_2, B_3, B_6 and folic acid.**

Without vitamins we would not be able to do anything – even thinking would be impossible. They are essential to hundreds of chemical reactions that go on inside our bodies the whole time, and they play an important role in preventing disease.

Most vitamins cannot be made by the body and must, therefore, be provided by our diet. The exceptions are niacin (vitamin B_3), small amounts of which can be made from the amino acid tryptophan; vitamin D, which is made by the action of sunlight on the skin; and biotin and vitamin K, which are made by bacteria in the intestine.

Vitamins can be divided into two groups: water-soluble vitamins (B complex and C); and fat-soluble ones (A, D, E, K). The water-soluble vitamins are very easily destroyed during the processing, storage, preparation and cooking of food. The fat-soluble vitamins are less vulnerable to losses during cooking and processing.

Our bodies are capable of storing some vitamins (A, B_{12}, D, E and K); the rest need to be provided by our diet on a regular basis. The government has set recommended daily intakes (Reference Nutrient Intakes or RNIs) for each vitamin, which correspond to the daily amount that should be sufficient to meet the needs of specified groups of individuals. A well-balanced diet that contains a wide variety of foods should provide all the vitamins you need to meet these recommended intakes, but there may be certain times in your life when you would benefit from taking a vitamin supplement.

Vitamin A (retinol)

Vitamin A is essential for normal growth, an efficient immune system, healthy skin and good vision. Deficiency is rare in western countries, but it is a major cause of blindness in much of the developing world. A very high intake of vitamin A – more than ten times the recommended levels – can be toxic. A high intake during pregnancy has been linked with birth defects, so pregnant women should avoid taking vitamin A supplements and eating liver, which is very high in the vitamin.

Beta carotene, the plant form of vitamin A, is a pigment found in brightly coloured and dark green fruit and vegetables. The body converts beta carotene into vitamin

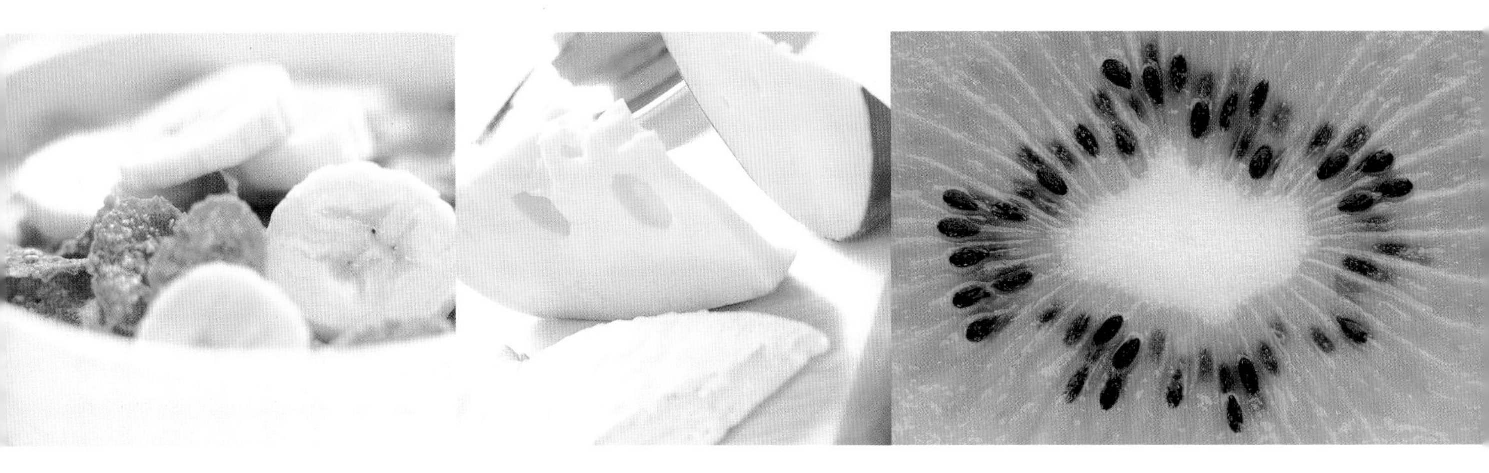

A, which, as an antioxidant, helps prevent damage to cells by free radicals, thereby protecting against heart disease and cancer. Taking more than the recommended levels of beta carotene can sometimes cause yellowing of the skin. This is completely harmless and the effect gradually disappears after the intake is reduced.

The B complex vitamins

There are eight vitamins in this group, and they are all water-soluble. Many of the B vitamins occur together in the same foods.

Vitamin B_1 (thiamin)

Thiamin is essential in the release of energy from carbohydrates. Deficiency is rare in the UK, but sometimes occurs in alcoholics.

Vitamin B_2 (riboflavin)

Like thiamin, riboflavin is vital for the release of energy from food. It's also essential for growth and helps maintain a healthy skin. Riboflavin is fairly stable when heated, but losses can occur as a result of leaching into cooking water. (To offset the loss, use the cooking water to make gravies or sauces.) It is destroyed by daylight – milk left in the sun for several hours will lose most of its riboflavin.

Vitamin B_3 (niacin)

Niacin plays an important role in the release of energy from food. It also helps maintain the health of the skin, nerves and digestive system. The vitamin is not easily destroyed by heat, but significant amounts can leach into cooking water.

Vitamin B_5 (pantothenic acid)

Part of a coenzyme that enables the body to take energy from food, vitamin B_5 is involved in many metabolic reactions. Some vitamin B_5 is lost in cooking, if the temperature rises above boiling point.

Vitamin B_6 (pyridoxine)

Needed to release energy from protein, vitamin B_6 also helps to produce haemoglobin for red blood cells. Deficiency is very rare, and usually only occurs as a result of the long-term use of medication.

Breakfast cereals are often fortified with vitamins; cheese is a good source of vitamin B_{12} for vegetarians; and kiwi fruit are rich in vitamin C.

food note

Some groups of people may have increased requirements for one or more vitamins. They are:

1. **Young children and adolescents.**
2. **Pregnant and breast-feeding women.**
3. **Anyone who is elderly or housebound.**
4. **Smokers and heavy drinkers.**
5. **Anyone following a restrictive diet, including slimmers.**
6. **The chronically ill.**
7. **Vegans and some vegetarians.**

Mangetout are a source of vitamins B_5 and C; olives contain vitamin E; and eggs are rich in vitamins A, B_2, B_6, B_{12}, D and biotin.

avoid

1 Leaving milk exposed to daylight – up to 70 per cent of the riboflavin can be lost in this way.

2 Deep-frying, which destroys the vitamin E in vegetable oils.

3 Eating liver and taking vitamin A supplements if you are pregnant.

Some women find that high-dose vitamin B_6 supplements are helpful in relieving many of the symptoms associated with pre-menstrual tension (PMS).

Vitamin B_{12} (cyanocobalamin)

Essential for all growth, the formation of red blood cells and the maintenance of a healthy nervous system, this vitamin is found only in foods of animal origin, such as meat, fish, milk or eggs. Vegetarians who eat dairy products will get enough of this vitamin, but vegans need to include foods fortified with vitamin B_{12} in their diet or take a regular supplement.

Vitamin B_{12} is stable when heated but, in common with other B complex vitamins, losses can occur during cooking. A vitamin B_{12} deficiency can cause a type of ANAEMIA.

Folic acid (folate)

Essential in the manufacture of amino acids and red blood cells, folic acid is also needed for cell division and the breakdown of protein. Large amounts of folic acid can be lost during processing and cooking, since it is unstable at high temperatures and easily leaches into the cooking water.

Women likely to conceive should take folic acid supplements before conception and in the first weeks of pregnancy, as this can help to reduce the chances of having a baby with spina bifida. Folic acid deficiency can cause a type of ANAEMIA.

Biotin

Biotin is used in the release of energy from foods and for the processing of fats and cholesterol. In adults, biotin, unlike most other vitamins, can be made by bacteria that live in the intestine. As a result deficiency is extremely rare.

Vitamin C (ascorbic acid)

Vital for growth, vitamin C is essential for the formation of collagen (a protein necessary for healthy bones, teeth, gums, blood capillaries and all connective tissue). It plays an important role in healing wounds and fractures, and acts as an antioxidant, helping to protect against heart disease and certain types of cancer. In addition, vitamin C aids the absorption of iron from plant foods, such as leafy green vegetables.

Vitamin C is the least stable of all the vitamins and large amounts can be lost during the preparation and cooking of food. To preserve the maximum amount of the vitamin, all foods should be cooked in the minimum of water – or steamed or microwaved – for as short a time as possible and should be served immediately. Never leave vegetables standing in water. Whenever possible, use the cooking water for making gravy, stock or soup.

A deficiency of vitamin C can result in slow wound healing, reduced resistance to infection, bleeding gums and, in severe cases, scurvy – though this condition is rarely seen nowadays.

Vitamin D (cholecalciferol)

Essential for the absorption of calcium and for the formation of healthy teeth and bones, vitamin D also plays a role in maintaining a healthy nervous system. It occurs naturally in many foods. However, the body can also make vitamin D whenever the skin is exposed to sunlight (hence its nickname, 'the sunshine vitamin'). A deficiency of vitamin D can sometimes cause joint problems and brittle bones. Elderly people who are housebound often have low levels of vitamin D, because of poor food intake and lack of exposure to sunshine.

Vitamin E (tocopherols)

Vitamin E is not one, but a number of related compounds usually called tocopherols. They all function as antioxidants, which protect the body from damage by free radicals. The vitamin E in vegetable oils is destroyed by the very high temperatures used for deep-frying food.

Vitamin K

Essential for producing prothrombin, which causes blood to clot, vitamin K has been found to exist in three forms: one is obtained from foods derived from plants; the other two are made by the bacteria in the intestine. Deficiency is rare.

food note

Vitamin C is easily destroyed during storage, preparation and cooking. To minimise losses:

1 **Buy fruit and vegetables only when needed and store in a cool, dark place.**

2 **Choose cooking methods that require little or no water, such as microwaving, steaming or roasting.**

3 **Never leave vegetables standing in water.**

4 **Eat food as soon as possible after it has been prepared.**

vitamins

vitamin	good sources	what it does	daily needs	symptoms of deficiency
A (DERIVED FROM RETINOL IN ANIMAL FOODS, AND FROM BETA CAROTENE IN PLANT FOODS)	Animal sources: liver, milk, butter, cheese, egg yolks and oil-rich fish. Plant sources: orange-fleshed and dark green vegetables and fruits.	Vital for normal growth, skin, vision, immune system and mucous membranes (in the lining of the respiratory and urinary tracts). Beta carotene is thought to act as an antioxidant in the body, helping to protect against heart disease and cancer.	Men: 700mcg Women: 600mcg Breast-feeding women: 950mcg	Increased susceptibility to infection, vision problems and respiratory disorders. Excess in pregnancy can lead to risk of miscarriage and defects in the foetus.
B_1 (THIAMIN)	Fortified bread and cereals, whole grains, lean meat (especially pork), fish, potatoes, nuts and pulses.	Needed to release energy from carbohydrates, and to ensure healthy brain, nerve-cell and heart function.	Men: 1mg Women: 0.8mg	Fatigue, weakness, nerve damage and, at its most severe, heart failure. Deficiency sometimes occurs among alcoholics.
B_2 (RIBOFLAVIN)	Milk and other dairy products, lean meats, fortified bread and breakfast cereals.	Helps release energy from food and interacts with other B vitamins. Also needed to maintain healthy skin.	Men: 1.3mg Women: 1.1mg	Dry, sore lips, bloodshot eyes, dermatitis and mild anaemia.
B_3 (NIACIN)	Lean meat, fish, pulses, fortified breakfast cereals, potatoes and nuts.	Vital for conversion of food into energy. Also helps maintain healthy skin, nerves and digestive system.	Men: 1.7mg Women: 1.3mg	Fatigue, weakness, depression, skin rashes (especially when exposed to sunlight) and, in severe cases, dementia.
B_5 (PANTOTHENIC ACID)	Meat, vegetables, dried fruit and nuts.	Essential for the release of energy from food and the synthesis of certain body chemicals, including cholesterol and hormones.	3-7mg	Deficiency is rare. Symptoms include a tingling sensation and numbness in the toes.
B_6 (PYRIDOXINE)	Meat, poultry, fish, eggs, wholewheat bread and fortified cereals, nuts, soya beans and yeast extract.	Stimulates release of energy from proteins. Vital for the immune system and the formation of red blood cells. Also helps maintain a healthy nervous system.	Men: 1.4mg Women: 1.2mg	Deficiency is rare, but may result from long-term medication. Warning signs include anaemia, depression and confusion.

vitamin	good sources	what it does	daily needs	symptoms of deficiency
B_{12} (CYANOCOBALAMIN)	Meat, poultry, fish, dairy products, eggs and some fortified breakfast cereals.	Vital for growth, the formation of red blood cells and a healthy nervous system.	1.5mcg	Can cause a tingling sensation or numbness in the limbs, anaemia and degeneration of the nervous system.
FOLIC ACID (FOLATE)	Offal, dark green leafy vegetables, pulses, nuts, whole grains, fortified breakfast cereals and bread.	Important for cell division and the formation of DNA. Extra may be needed before conception and during pregnancy because the vitamin is vital to the growth of new cells. Also relieves depression in the elderly.	200mcg Pregnant women: 400mcg	Anaemia. Linked with birth defects such as spina bifida.
BIOTIN	Found in most foods. Especially abundant in liver, eggs, and fortified foods such as yeast extract.	Required to release energy from food, and for processing of fat and cholesterol.	10-200mcg	A normal diet supplies sufficient biotin. Dermatitis and hair loss are signs of deficiency in people with malabsorption problems.
C (ASCORBIC ACID)	Fruit and vegetables, especially citrus fruit, strawberries, kiwi fruit, tomatoes, peppers, broccoli and potatoes.	Necessary for the formation of collagen (essential for healthy gums, teeth, bones and skin). Aids healing of wounds and fractures and, as an antioxidant, may help protect against cancer and heart disease. Also boosts absorption of iron from plant food.	40mg Smokers: at least 80mg	Poor healing of wounds and lowered resistance to infection. Lethargy, reduced appetite, bleeding gums, scaly skin and aching joints.
D (CHOLECALCIFEROL)	Fortified dairy produce, oil-rich fish and fortified breakfast cereals.	Promotes absorption of calcium, necessary for normal development of bones and teeth.	People confined indoors: 10mcg	Soft and brittle bones, causing pain and fractures. In children, can lead to rickets.
E (TOCOPHEROLS)	Vegetable oils (such as corn and sunflower), wheatgerm, nuts, seeds and avocados.	As an antioxidant, helps to neutralise or destroy excess free radicals (unstable molecules that may cause cancer). Also helps protect against heart disease.	Men: at least 4mg Women: at least 3mg	Deficiency is rare, found only in those unable to absorb fat, and in premature babies. Symptoms include anaemia and nerve damage.
K (PHYLLOQUINONE, MENAQUINONE)	Dark green leafy vegetables such as cabbage, spinach, broccoli and Brussels sprouts.	Vital for normal blood clotting and making of some proteins. Involved in bone formation.	Men: 70mcg Women: 65mcg	Deficiency is rare in adults, and is usually caused by disease or medication. In advanced cases, can hinder normal blood clotting.

Nearly two-thirds of our body weight is water, so it is not surprising that it is essential for good health

water

benefits

1 **Essential for cell metabolism.**

2 **Promotes good digestion.**

3 **Flushes out toxins and waste products.**

4 **Drinking at least eight glasses daily will improve your vitality and the health of your skin.**

5 **Drinking plenty of water reduces the risk of cystitis, bladder infections, kidney stones, constipation and headaches.**

6 **The bubbles in carbonated water can alleviate morning sickness.**

drawbacks

1 **Tap water may contain chemical residues.**

2 **The bubbles in carbonated water can aggravate irritable bowel syndrome and indigestion.**

Water is vital to thousands of chemical processes that take place in the body's cells to enable it to function. It is needed to regulate body temperature and to lubricate joints and eyes. It enables the body to draw nutrients from food and drink, and by flushing out the kidneys it helps the body get rid of toxins and waste products.

About a third of an adult's daily fluid intake is provided by food, the rest from drinks such as tea, coffee, fruit juices and fizzy drinks. But for optimum health, nutritionists advise drinking 2–2.5 litres (3–5 pints) of water daily, limiting tea, coffee and cola drinks to three a day because they contain dehydrating diuretics.

Anxiety about the quality of our tap water in recent years has fuelled a surge in the sales of water filters and bottled waters, but experts remain divided over whether such precautions are necessary. The risks of lead poisoning from old water pipes are minimal today as most have been replaced, but it is still wise – especially in soft-water areas – to run the cold water tap for a few seconds each morning to run off water that has lain overnight in the pipes. Fluoride is added to water supplies in some areas to protect against tooth decay, but scientists are still researching its effects. Whether oestrogen-like chemicals in water supplies could reduce male fertility is also being investigated by scientists.

Water filters remove chemicals present in tap water, but they cannot extract them all, and some may take out beneficial minerals such as calcium and magnesium as well.

Bottled waters are believed to be healthier than tap water, but they are not invariably so. ('Spring' or 'table' waters can legally come from any source, ranging from natural springs to tap water.) There is no limit on nitrate levels in mineral water (50mg per litre in tap water). And while some mineral waters have valuable quantities of calcium and magnesium, others are high in sodium so should be avoided by anyone with high blood pressure. Many actually contain no more minerals than tap water, but are unlikely to contain chemical residues. On balance, there may be little to choose between tap and bottled water healthwise, but the distinctive tastes of the different bottled varieties win them many devotees.

yeast extract

Containing potassium, magnesium and zinc, yeast extract is above all an excellent source of B vitamins, needed for energy release and a healthy metabolism and nervous system. In particular, it is a good source of folic acid, vital just before and during pregnancy. Some yeast extracts are fortified with vitamin B_{12}, making them invaluable for vegans, as B_{12} occurs almost exclusively in foods of animal origin.

Yeast extract is high in sodium, so anyone who has high blood pressure or is following a low-sodium diet should eat it sparingly. However, it is worth remembering that one slice of toast is likely to contain more sodium that the average amount of yeast extract spread on it - and many low-salt versions are now available.

Some practitioners of alternative medicine claim that foods containing yeast aggravate THRUSH and its extreme form, systemic candidiasis, by inhibiting the growth of 'friendly' bacteria in the gut and letting *Candida albicans* (which causes thrush) proliferate. However, this theory is not widely accepted by orthodox medicine.

benefits

1 **Superb source of most B vitamins, including folic acid.**

2 **Contains potassium, magnesium and zinc.**

3 **May be fortified with vitamin B_{12}, making it a valuable element in a vegan diet.**

drawback

High sodium content.

yogurt

Many people who cannot digest milk can obtain calcium from yogurt, which also provides phosphorus for healthy teeth and bones, and vitamins B_2 (riboflavin) and B_{12}.

Greek yogurt has 115 Calories in a 100g (3½oz) portion, twice as many as low-fat plain yogurt; whole-milk plain yogurt has about 80. Fruit yogurts have a lot of added sugar, which boosts their calorie content.

'Live' yogurt contains *Lactobacillus acidophilus* among other bacterial cultures, and has health benefits that are now being recognised by scientists. It discourages the proliferation of harmful bacteria and yeasts (including *Candida albicans*) in the gut which can cause bowel infections. It helps to relieve constipation and diarrhoea, too, as well as bad breath caused by digestive disorders. Also, applying yogurt to the skin can help to clear up yeast infections, such as THRUSH.

One common side effect of antibiotics is that they deplete the levels of 'friendly' bacteria in the gut. A daily portion of live yogurt helps to restore these bacteria, thereby re-establishing the body's defences.

benefits

1 **Useful source of calcium, phosphorus and B vitamins.**

2 **Helps to ward off gastro-intestinal infections, and candidiasis.**

3 **Helps to restore 'friendly' bacteria in the gut and boost the body's immune system.**

useful numbers

Alcohol Concern
Waterbridge House,
32-36 Loman Street,
London SE1 0EE
(0207 928 7377)

Alzheimer's Society
Gordon House,10 Greencoat
Place, London SW1P 1PH
(0845 300 0336)

Anaphylaxis Campaign
PO Box 149, Fleet, Hampshire
GU13 0FA (01252 542 029)

Arthritic Association
First Floor Suite,
2 Hyde Gardens, Eastbourne,
East Sussex BN21 4PN

British Allergy Foundation
Deepdene House,
30 Belle Grove Road, Welling,
Kent DA16 3PY (0208 303 8583)

British College of Naturopathy and Osteopathy
Fraser House, 13 Netherhall
Gardens, London NW3 5RR
(0207 435 7830)

British Dental Health Association
Word of Mouth Patient Hotline
(0870 333 1188)
St Peter's Road, Rugby,
Warwickshire CV21 3QP

British Diabetic Association
10 Queen Anne Street, London
W1M 0BD (0207 323 1531)

British Heart Foundation
14 Fitzhardinge Street,
London W1H 4DH
(0207 935 0185)

British Nutrition Foundation
High Holborn House,
52-54 High Holborn,
London WC1V 6RQ
(0207 404 6504)

Cancer Research Campaign
10 Cambridge Terrace,
London NW1 4JL
(0207 224 1333)

Coeliac Society
PO Box 220, High Wycombe,
Bucks HP11 2HY
(01494 437 278)

Cystic Fibrosis Trust
11 London Road, Bromley,
Kent BR1 1BY (0208 464 7211)

Department of Health
Richmond House,
79 Whitehall,
London SW1A 2NS
(0207 210 3000)

Hyperactive Children's Support Group
71 Whyke Lane, Chichester,
West Sussex PO19 2LD
(01903 725 182)

IBS Nutrition Advice
32 Trent Court,
New Wanstead,
London E11 2TF (0208 989 1812)

Imperial Cancer Research Fund
PO Box 123, Lincoln's Inn Fields,
London WC2A 3PX
(0207 242 0200)

Migraine Action Association
178A High Road, Byfleet,
Surrey KT14 7ED
(01932 352 468)

National Association for Colitis and Crohn's Disease
4 Beaumont House, Sutton Road,
St Albans, Herts AL1 5HH
(01727 844 296)

National Asthma Campaign
Helpline (0845 701 0203)
Providence House,
Providence Place,
London N1 0NT

National Candida Society
PO Box 151, Orpington,
Kent BR5 1UJ (01689 813 039)
(Thurs-Sat,10am-4pm)

National Childbirth Trust
Alexandra House,
Oldham Terrace, London
W3 6NH (0208 992 8637)

National Osteoporosis Society
PO Box 10, Radstock,
Bath BA3 3YB (01761 472 721)

Vegetarian Society
Parkdale, Dunham Road,
Altrincham, Cheshire
WA14 4QG (0161 925 2000)

picture credits

Trevor Vaughan: front cover (bl), 1, 3, 6, 15, 19, 23 (tr), 24 (t), 25, 27, 28 (bl), 30, 44, 51, 89, 94, 96, 131, 138, 142, 150, 156, 167, 170, 176, back cover.
Images Colour Library: front cover (tl, tr, br), 16, 23 (br), 24, 41, 69, 71, 101, 112 (tr), 159.
Tony Stone Images: 5, 21, 23 (tl, bc), 24, 29, 30, 33, 35, 36, 38, 45, 48, 54 (bc), 59 (bl), 65, 74, 90, 102, 109, 111 (tc), 112 (tc), 119, 121, 128, 149, 165 (tl).
Steve Baxter: 8, 9.
Telegraph Col Library: 11, 12, 17 (bg, bl), 20, 43, (bg, bl), 54 (bg), 59 (bg), 64, 76, 82, 84-85, 92, 105, 116, 117, 154 (bg, bc), 162.
Imagebank: 23 (bl), 24, 53, 55, 86, 103, 106, 111 (tl), 122, 140, 165 (tc), 166.
Cephas: 26, 99, 111 (tr), 144.
Food Features: 28 (tl).
Tesco Recipe Magazine: 32, 62, 82, 112 (tl), 124, 130, 145, 152-153, 166 (tr).
Anthony Blake: 52, 60, 77, 79, 113, 127, 141, 166 (tl).
Superstock: 93, 136.
Julian Cotton: 97.
Moose Azim: 132.
Abbreviations: bg=background, b=bottom, c=centre, l=left, r=right, t=top.
Picture Research: **Rizwan Mirza**

To protect the identity of the people in the case studies, models have been used for all the pictures – they are not the actual people described.

index

Page numbers in bold type refer to main entries.

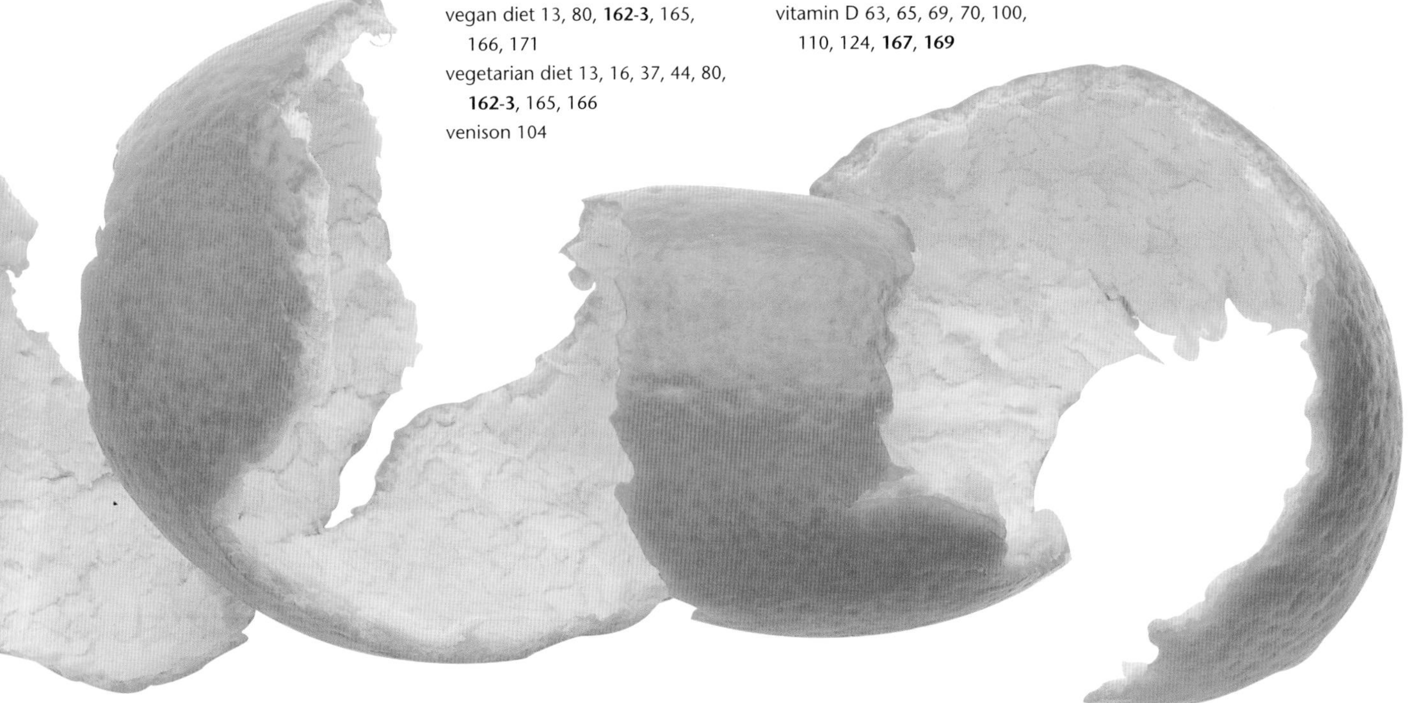